always
a little
further

Jack Swaab, March 2016. (*Photograph by Andrew McDonald*)

always
a little
further
reflections from
late in the day

An Updated 100th Birthday Edition

We are the Pilgrims, master; we shall go
Always a little further; it may be
Beyond that last blue mountain barred with snow
Across that angry or that glimmering sea.

James Elroy Flecker, *Hassan*

JACK SWAAB

FONTHILL

Thanks to my sons for helpful comments and encouraging me to write the book,
to Andrew McDonald for author and cat photos,
and to Camilla Hill for typing and 'civilising' my handwritten version.

By the same author:

Field of Fire: Diary of a Gunner Officer (Sutton Publishing, 2005)
Slouching in the Undergrowth (Fonthill Media, 2012)
The Ninth Life of Bella Simkins (eBook, 2015)

Fonthill Media Limited
www.fonthillmedia.com
office@fonthillmedia.com

First published in the United Kingdom 2016
Second edition published 2018

British Library Cataloguing in Publication Data:
A catalogue record for this book is available from the British Library

ISBN 978-1-78155-583-5

Typeset in 10.5pt on 13pt Sabon
Printed and bound in England

PREFACE

The first edition of this book, published in 2016, ended with entry 91, written at the end of 2015. The new, enlarged edition continues with further reflections written between the authors 99th birthday on 15 March 2017 and New Year's Eve 2017. It is published to celebrate his 100th birthday on 15 March 2018.

1

2013

I never expected to achieve my biblical quota of three score years and ten. So I was surprised—amazed, even—to see in the new century at *four* score years (not to mention a one-year bonus). What to think then as I head deep into the Nineties (born 1918)? If life bowls me a few long hops outside the leg stump, that unlikely Elysian scoreboard will be preparing three unthought-of figures.

So what? I hear you asking; and it's a good question. Why do I feel this urge to commit to paper my experience of life and my increasingly grumpy opinions? And why should I think anyone else (family excepted, perhaps) would be interested?

2

2014

Thinking about it, I suppose that writing has always been a sort of addiction for me. Even at kindergarten I was noted for "composition" and later edited my school magazine and co-founded a magazine, *Fords and Bridges*, during my ill-fated sojourn at Oxford. Later I was a reporter and slightly overblown feature writer for *Cavalcade* the national magazine ("Marijuana, the scourge of youth").

I still have a few short stories I wrote in occupied Germany in 1945 and thereafter my advertising career started as a copywriter and developed as a creative writer and manager.

It was due solely to the interest of my great-nephew, Simon, that my first book (a wartime diary) found a publisher when I was 87 years old and this ignited that urge to write once more, with the additional and pleasurable incentive of being published again in my nineties. So this has turned out to be my fourth book, including my children's e-book which I published in 2015.

I have to regard writing as in some sense a substitute for failing physical powers; and myself fortunate still to retain the ability to communicate with the world around me. And, as my other books have in their own way defined aspects of my earlier life, so I attempt in this one to comment on some events of these final years and here and there look back on memories they provide.

3

If, in reply to the question I raised above, you *are* interested, I have to admit that, as I grow older, I am often (usually) so tired. Especially after my daily walk. I remember the time when I arrived home ready for some pressing task, where now I slump in an armchair with an aching back and wistful thoughts of my electric blanket. (And I fear that this blameless accessory may conk out one of these days if I keep forgetting to switch it off when I get up—having stealthily switched it on at 3 a.m. in search of heat-inducing sleep.)

Getting up, yes. As soon as I remove my pyjama jacket I feel a furry body rub against me. It's Mina, my new tabby lady given me (for Christmas) by my elder son Richard after my beautiful Rainbow was run over and killed three months ago. I hope to tell you about cats in my life at some point in this narrative.

4

People often talk to me nowadays about reaching a hundred as though it is some sort of target. (As, indeed, I have treated it myself a few lines above.) But what really matters is your health—and, with that, comes your independence. What's the point of just being around if you can't *do* anything?

5

Wouldn't it be awful if I've been wrong all this time and there really is some sort of C of E Heaven? I see myself hustled by winged escorts into the august presence and questioned about my life and times. The Ten Commandments:

'Well, Sir, I'm afraid, thinking about it, that I've broken most of them.'

'*Most?*'

'Fraid so, Sir.'

' Well it's no use standing there snivelling. Why no worshipping the Lord your God, i.e. Me?'

'Well you see Sir, I didn't believe that you existed. I was what they called an atheist, though I did belong to the agnostic tendency.'

'A pretty poor record.... Take him down (this to the angelic guards) while I consider suitable retribution for this sorry specimen.'

6

Today, January 2015, is Holocaust Memorial Day, which has triggered my never much absent thoughts about death, God etc. There's no two ways about it. If God is omnipotent, he comes across as incompetent, indifferent or downright nasty. If you believe in God (or anyway the Christian version) you have to ask yourself: 'is there forgiveness for Hitler and his murderous accomplices?' Not to mention Stalin, Pol Pot among so many. I'd love to ask the Pope or Archbishop Welby that question. No doubt they'd have an answer of sorts but then you have to remind yourself that if you could devise a vessel to travel into space at 100,000 mph, it could take you forty years to reach the nearest star in our universe in all its immensity. And our universe is only one of many universes … at which point the whole concept of God as expressed by man's major religions becomes so absurd as to be unable to grasp. So the conversational tone of the prayers to which I listen on Radio 4 on Sundays (I enjoy the hymns which I, myself, sang for years in the choir at school) is really ludicrous—particularly for some reason which I can't quite fathom—when intoned by one of the token Lady reverends.

7

I sometimes think that the thing which really spooks me about death is the way it sneaks up on you and catches you by surprise. Would it be better if you could find out the time and place of your departure? Or would the knowledge of your remaining time become increasingly disturbing? And there's another thing: if your vision of departure saw it as comfortable and pleasant; in your own home, say, with your little cat's furry warmth to speed you on your way, that might be acceptable. But what if you were to meet one of many violent ends and depart howling with pain and misery? Maybe it's better, after all, to be caught unawares. What gloomy thoughts for a gloomy rain-sodden Sunday.

8

Oh dear. Maybe it's been the incessant rain and bad weather, but the gloominess mentioned above, has continued lately. I find myself on my daily walk, reciting the sonnet "Rendezvous with Death" by that unfortunate young Canadian killed as The Great War neared its end. "When Spring comes back with rustling shade / And apple blossoms fill the air / When Spring brings back blue days and fair" he wrote. Alan Seeger doesn't seem to be in many anthologies so I'd like to include the poem which I've always felt reflected the hopes and fears of the young soldiers of the First World War:

> *I have a rendezvous with Death*
> *At some disputed barricade,*
> *When Spring comes back with rustling shade*
> *And apple-blossoms fill the air—*
> *I have a rendezvous with Death*
> *When Spring brings back blue days and fair.*

> *It may be he shall take my hand*
> *And lead me into his dark land*
> *And close my eyes and quench my breath—*
> *It may be I shall pass him still.*
> *I have a rendezvous with Death*
> *On some scarred slope of battered hill*
> *When Spring comes round again this year*
> *And the first meadow-flowers appear.*

> *God knows 'twere better to be deep*
> *Pillowed in silk and scented down,*
> *Where Love throbs out in blissful sleep,*
> *Pulse nigh to pulse, and breath to breath,*
> *Where hushed awakenings are dear ....*
> *But I've a rendezvous with Death*
> *At midnight in some flaming town,*
> *When Spring trips north again this year,*
> *And I to my pledged word am true,*
> *I shall not fail that rendezvous.*

My mood has not been lightened by reading an item in today's paper, stating that now drugs aren't going to be "wasted" on the elderly. I suppose, to be objective (not all that easy) it does make sense but we weren't always elderly. And those remaining few thousand of us who underwent what Julian Grenfell called "the thundering line of battle" not once but many times, don't we deserve some medical "thank you" (for what won't probably be long)?

9

I suppose that an old thing like me should not allow himself to be irritated by some really trivial things. Although, perhaps, this is the time of life when it's acceptable. I'm not talking here of the various stages of dislike, disgust and positive hatred exemplified by, say, Mugabe, Jong Un, George Galloway, Ken Livingstone and Alex Salmond, nor to forget the evil creatures seen in TV documentaries, Hitler, Himmler etc.

No. Just irritating things like the whistle at the end of the McDonald's ads. Then there is a certain newsreader. I mean, I like my news read in English, not for example "Tox about wukking in Oggust". Another thing: what I call the "When eyes": when I was Minister of whatever, when I was Mayor of wherever. "I don't want to know" I shout at the radio / TV. Also, people (though I don't dispute their right) who persist in calling it "two thousand and fourteen" instead of "twenty fourteen". Do you think they were saying "one thousand nine hundred and fourteen" just before The Great War? I ought really to write a poem which would be the opposite of Rupert Brooke's *The Great Lover*, or Julie Andrews's *Favourite Things*, but I don't think I've the energy (or, indeed, the ability).

The sun has come out and my tabby cat, Mina, sprawls contentedly on my sunlit duvet. Time to cheer up, perhaps. But before I do: just add those drivers who don't raise a "Thank You" hand when you've given way in a crowded and ambiguous traffic situation.

10

Yesterday was the warmest day of the year and my daily walk was blessed with welcome sunshine. The only downside was very persistent backache—the legacy of an otherwise successful laminectomy operation in 2006. It put me in mind of a dear friend who endures a very much worse back condition with a great deal less fuss than me (or do I mean I? I'm never quite sure). Life has treated her so inconsistently. Blessed with beauty, charm and a wonderful laugh, a successfully decorated, distinguished (knighted) husband who died much too soon. But plagued by increasing back pain, finally beyond surgery, and, a voracious reader, forced to spend much of her later years lying in bed with her books.

11

I know I banged on about this in my last book, but the recent weather has brought it all (rather appropriately) flooding back. I refer, of course, to the stealthy way in which the weather forecasters have introduced—though not consistently—what I called snooty Celsius and metric measurement. This applies particularly to rain or snowfall quoted in millimetres or centimetres or now and then "an inch of rain". I have learned to talk about thirty-two degrees now but it hasn't the reality of sweaty old ninety, has it?

Nobody seems to know whether these two systems have been legally introduced (like the switchover to decimal money) or just inflicted upon us without any consultation. I suppose I'm an old reactionary but funnily enough I would welcome adoption of the twenty four hour clock which, of course, I used in my army years. I understand about the meridian of course but there *are* 24 hours in the day, so why not recognise it?

12

One day last week, the spring sunshine seemed unusually warm and for some reason, I kept thinking of certain other sunny days in my past. After the war, my regiment was stationed in a town in Germany called Verden on Aller. The Aller part was the small, clear, fast-flowing river on the edge of town. I spent that blissful summer of '45 (freed from the recent attempts on my life) swimming from time to time in the river. I'd walk upstream and then float down, swim to the bank and lie drying in the grass. Then there was my best friend Mervyn's villa in the Algarve. We swam, naked in his pool and then lay in the deckchairs needing no towel, dried by the warm Portuguese sun.

Another memory was vividly stirred earlier in my life as I lay in hospital cocooned and helpless after a spinal operation. I remember how I kept visualising those past years when I pranced in the sunlit surf of Porthcothan Bay; and—I write this with some shame—I remember weeping weakly for my lost years. (I went back to Porthcothan last year and it was as wonderful as ever—but covered in a sea mist which only added to the enduring magic of the place.)

13

I've just been reading about a Mr Trotter who has won £107 million on the National Lottery. Far from envying him, I would just hate to win that sort of money. (Not that I will, because I don't spend money on something offering such impossible odds against a win.) Mr Trotter, now fourth on the Rich List, is going to start by buying a McLaren Super Car, first of a fleet of expensive models. Well, one car OK, or even two, or three at a pinch. But a fleet? Of course, I'm too old to enjoy the worldly pleasures which come with such a huge sum. But how it would distort everything. What on earth to do with it? I'd enjoy, say, £50,000. Just enough to give a good sum to people who wouldn't expect it. Enough to get the house re-wired and maybe join BUPA. The numerous charities I support with small donations (animals, small African children, rough sleepers, cancer fighters etc.) I'd support with large donations. (I dare say Mr Trotter, who seems a pleasant sort of chap, will do much the same but on a much larger scale. Good luck to him.)

14

I look at my new clock radio (birthday present from Richard). "3.50 SU". My god, I meant to go for a walk. Wait a minute, you *did* go. Oh yes, I remember now. I've had a nap like my little cat, Mina, sprawled on the sunlit sofa. In a children's book I've written, I feature as an old man who has been a cat in a previous life; as I feel myself to have been. However, I didn't mean to discuss all that.

I've been brooding on how—doubtless an aspect of old age—sort of repelled I feel by the obsession with food and drink which dominates so much of the media. I've never been at all dependent on booze, though I've been drunk many times, especially in the war and after in the ad business (when, successful, I had my own drinks cupboard). And I recall one night in Portugal when Mervyn and I got quite disgracefully drunk. I drove our hired Mini through the soft Algarve night, foot flat to the floor, our wives screaming in terror. My ancient self looks back on this episode with disapproval and disgust.

15

No, what I find particularly off-putting are those cooking competitions. It's the part where the judges sample the dishes and pronounce their verdict. There's something so really repellent about the way they chew and chomp. I seem to hear disgusting imaginary slurping noises as they salivate. Of course, the cooks are very ingenious as they concoct elaborate dishes but I'm reminded of the almost daily appeals I receive for starving people and

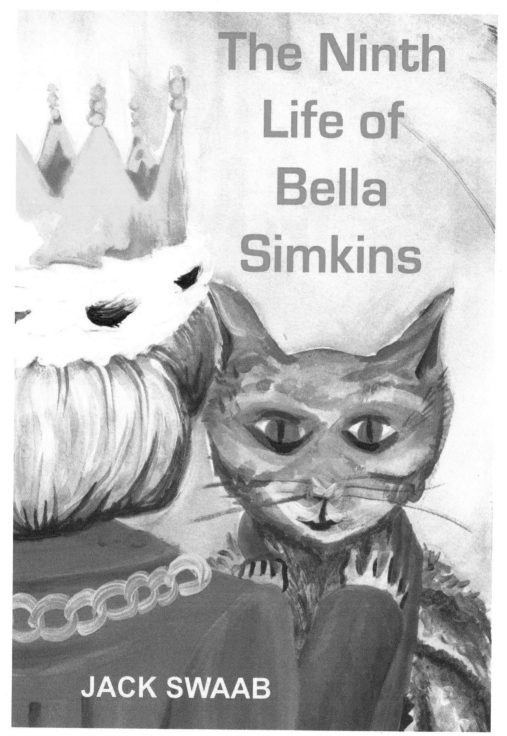

Jack Swaab's children's book, *The Ninth Life of Bella Simkins* (2015)—see amazon.co.uk/website. Cover artwork by Andrew McDonald.

infants who die for lack of clean water and something—anything—to eat. I used to have a scotch and dry ginger every evening before supper. (Zena often shared it. "Sippers" I'd tell her "not *gulpers*".) I gave this up because my doctor suggested that a small single should be my limit, and that hardly moistened the glass. I've never been all that keen on wine and although I can just about identify a smooth claret from a thin acid-y one, I find so much of the wine writing really ridiculous. I remember there used to be a blonde lady on TV who was beyond parody. And this, in a recent copy of my *Spectator* describing a sherry as having "that fino teeth-on-edge flirtiness, plus subtlety and length". Would that tempt you to try it? Would you even have any idea what it meant?

But about food. I've always been unadventurous, with a few much enjoyed meals like a well-fried Dover sole with lemon butter, or a roast leg of lamb (carved inward towards the bone). Zena used to give me the same birthday supper year after year (as requested): duck and "words" (of one syllabub). So I may be gastronomically boring but I'm not a glutton.

16

I suppose that somebody somewhere has done some research on this: whether all old people living alone talk to their pets. I've always talked to my cats. More, I have answered for them. Conversation tends to concern the day I first saw them, what I said, the head-rubs and the unlikely thought (in *their* minds) that they would be lying stretched out upon me as I watch TV from my bed. They then respond in a rather high pitched voice which I feel suitable for lady cats. Sometimes they purr but as I'm very deaf in one ear, I usually have to rely on the whirring that throbs against me. This is particularly true of Mina, my present cat, who has a quiet purr which is rather sparingly allocated, unlike Rainbow, her immediate predecessor, alas run over one black October day, and Bella who preceded *her*. I think my feline dialogues have been helped by work I put in on the *Commando* comics I used to buy the boys when they were boys. They liked to be read to and I became rather a convincingly guttural Nazi parachutist or Japanese Kamikaze pilot, depending on the subject matter of that week's issue. These little books had a menacing commando knife on the cover and were rather well drawn. I continue to hope that the large number we had may be in the loft with some of the other books for which there was no house at the time. I might try to find out whether they would fetch a few quid on eBay. Things do. A man came into the bookshop where I worked on my first retirement job and—I can't quite recall how the subject arose—offered to buy the rather exotic collection of hotel labels I'd collected on my travels. I think he paid me twenty pounds, which seemed quite generous. I since have a duplicate set: Shephards, Raffles etc.).

17

Driving home along Moorgate recently, I stopped at a red light. Fenchurch Street on my left, Lombard Street on my right. Eighty-odd years ago, I used to go to 48 Fenchurch Street in the school holidays, where my father was waiting to take me to lunch at The Lombard Grill. As we walked there my father must have been greeted by a couple of dozen fellow workers. After thirty five or more years working in the City (five and a half days a week) he was a small, well-known character. At the Lombard, waiters wheeled in trolleys containing substantial joints of meat covered by imposing silvery domes. They carved the meat with ferocious knives. It was all rather unusual and treatsome.

The last time I went there was on leave just after the war ended. I remember how proud Dad was of a soldier son with medal ribbons on his chest. I hoped it made up for my rather disappointing beginnings.

18

With old age sensual pleasures fade away (as John Betjeman ruefully recalled). Or, as the preacher puts it in the book of Ecclesiastes "Desire shall fail; because man goeth to his long home ..." and, earlier, contemplating bodily failure: "The strong men shall bow themselves, and the grinders cease because they are few, and those that look out of the windows be darkened".

I love Ecclesiastes and frequently turn to it in Zena's tattered family Bible, first given to her forbear Edward Binney Laing in 1890. It contains some of the most beautiful sentences in the English Language albeit couched in a somewhat gloomy mood. But how many people could tell you that "Cast your bread upon the waters etc." comes from this very source? As I say, like many atheists I love much of the Bible and indeed "Remember now thy creator ..." appears on page one of my first book; and was read by Richard at Zena's funeral service.

And, perhaps, will be at mine. If I have a funeral. Funerals? The thing I actually intended to describe as a remaining pleasure was one of the real, tangible ones I still enjoy. On Saturday night I have a very warm shower and wash my hair. Dried and powdered I don my radiator-heated pyjamas. Then, on with my dressing gown and down on my bed (I've changed the bedding that morning) where I lie, blissfully cocooned to watch some deplorable TV programme with its mandatory warnings: "Contains violence, strong language" and "scenes of a SEXUAL NATURE" which "some viewers may find disturbing". This viewer, not unduly disturbed, tumbles into a welcoming bed, puts out the light and, tabby-comforted, drifts off to sleep.

19

Some years ago, Zena and I heard a talk on the radio, given, I think by one of the family who lived at Knole; Vita Sackville-West. What made a lasting impression on us was how, in the autumn, they used to wade through mounds of dried leaves; and the pleasure this gave them, they described as "walking through leaves". Zena and I extrapolated this to other small but telling pleasures. In particular, I remember the moment when you're peeling a hardboiled egg and a whole chunk of the shell detaches itself from the shiny slippery body within. Also pleasing is the sound of a coin settling on a hard surface—a kitchen unit say—with that kind of mad whirring sound which seems to go on and on till it subsides like the end of a sneeze. A similar effect can be obtained with a jam jar lid, but it lacks the high pitched élan of (in the old days) a half-crown or florin.

I know that there were other examples, but these are the ones that have stuck in my memory and, indeed, are still enjoyed, though today's coinage is not as robust as those I grew up with. (And yes, I am ending with a preposition.)

20

I suppose it's inevitable as you grow older and older, that the cruelty in the world plays more and more on your mind. In my case, the thing I can hardly bear to think about is cruelty to animals. I simply cannot comprehend the mind of people who capture bears to make them dance by ringing their delicate noses. I'd not be disturbed to see the death sentence for such people. I suppose my life has been influenced by some of my reading. Sometime, probably in the thirties I was deeply influenced by Masefield's great poem "Reynard the Fox". And although I sympathise with my friend whose chickens are ruthlessly destroyed—not eaten—by a local fox, I could never bring myself to hunt one; or, for that matter, shoot a bird. But hypocrite that I am, I eat pheasant and grouse and other winged victims. As Blake wrote "A robin redbreast in a cage / Puts all Heaven in a rage". Ralph Hodgson, too, in his poem, "The Bells of Heaven" imagines a congregation kneeling "with angry prayers / For tamed and shabby tigers / And dancing dogs and bears / And wretched, blind pit ponies / And little hunted hares".

Hodgson is a poet I much admire. His moving poem "The Bull" stayed with me for long after I read it. Indeed, the title of my second book *Slouching in the Undergrowth* comes from the opening lines of that poem. Nowadays I am sickened and enraged by TV pictures of elephants and rhinos slaughtered by poachers who hack off their tusks to make money in the illegal ivory market. When I talk of the death penalty it is these people and those who cut off the paws of tigers, that I have in mind. And the people who cut the fins off sharks to make soup and leave the wretched, beautiful, creatures to die, helpless.

My daily life is haunted to a greater or lesser degree by the wrong that is done to creatures who have no defence; and I haven't even mentioned the small mice and little monkeys who live out their short, sacrificial lives in our laboratories. Shame on us all!

21

Do you ever watch Party Conferences? I used to, until, like some Amazonian monkey hit by a curare-laden arrow I became paralysed with boredom and disgust. Imagine being a delegate, trained to clap as the Leader spoke and produce the mandatory standing ovation when he (or she) finished. And have you watched as some Cabinet colleague is singled out for praise? The cameras linger on the favoured one who sniggers with struggling hubris and false modesty. The rest of the front row clap furiously and display their murderous smiles. I remember how I spotted my one-time Board colleague, Bill Shelton ("False fleeting perjured Clarence") as he glanced furtively at those about him before deciding to get to his feet for the ovation. He must have targeted his tongue accurately as he duly received his K. I thought the acme of sycophancy was reached when Mrs Thatcher hooted "You turn if you want to but the La-a-a-a-dy's not for turning". This mildly amusing paraphrase (probably not even identified by most of the delegates) was greeted with braying, with howling, with truly orgasmic delight. I imagine that the speechwriter flushed with pleasure and I wondered whether Mrs T, who reputedly did not enjoy a GSOH, was a bit baffled by the pandemonium she'd triggered.

I admit to one occasional look these days, but—especially when some pointless Lib-Dem is holding forth—tend to reach for the off button on my remote. And, talking of Lib-Dems, who can fail to enjoy the final exhortation of David now Lord Steele to "prepare for government".

In your dreams, My Lord, the mouse that roared.

22

Talking of reactions: some years ago, I was asked how I'd felt about some allegedly humorous show. I replied "Like one of those huge stone-faced statues on Easter Island" or "a blank wooden-faced cigar stone Indian". Nowadays my response to any show I find unfunny is "Easter Island".

23

I wondered the other day: how many cat books have I got? It's twenty. Some are quite small by famous ailurophiles like Doris Lessing, A. L. Rowse, Paul Gallico and—high on the list of my all-time favourite books—"Charles" by Michael Joseph. It has a heart-breaking ending; but then isn't it always when one's furry friend departs?

I've always tried to share those last moments. Usually the friend has jumped quickly back into the cat basket I used to have, curled up and gone to the sleep from which there was no wakening. I remember as I sat racked with grief as my adopted Persian Mr Grey departed, Jim Sinclair, my vet for many years (though now retired) said to me "There are worse ways to go". I thought yes that's true and consoling. It's the way I'd like to go if the right situation arose. Not legal, alas.

Even so, I now lack the courage to be there at the end. So I failed Bella, my little 24-7 companion for so many years. I dare say—I hope—she forgave me.

24

It's the 6th of June tomorrow and the TV is full of pictures of events over the Channel. I look up the entry in *Field of Fire* for 1944 and see that I was sailing for Normandy—greeted by the big German guns at Gris Nez which blew up the ship two behind us with a huge column of smoke and flame. Actually I didn't arrive (at Sword beach) till the next day, and was lucky enough to get a cushy landing (as we had in Sicily when we were almost the first troops ashore). But what my old CO2 used to call the "'ot shit" arrived soon enough. Ten years ago I was invited to the 60th anniversary at the Imperial War Museum. Someone in the know told me that the Normandy Veterans' Association had rather hijacked the occasion; and I have to say that most of the "heroes" I met certainly weren't the ones who faced the shellfire and bullets at Juno, Sword and Gold beaches on that summer morning three score and ten years ago. Or, for that matter, anywhere else....

25

"The world is too much with us" wrote William Wordsworth. "Getting and spending" he added, "we lay waste our powers".

In 2014, only one word—the third is missing: The World Cup. On TV today, I saw a chap who had saved £100 a month for two years to go to Brazil. I simply cannot relate to the mindset of this. Perhaps I've never felt that sort of fanatical attachment to sporting events. Mind you, I've not been without my own loyalties. I stood on the terraces at Highbury to support Arsenal for many a Saturday afternoon in the thirties (costing a few pence I seem to recall). And on a rather grander scale (having sat on the grass for test matches at The Oval as a small boy), I became a member of the MCC where, thanks to my friendship with Colonel J. W. A. Stephenson, I was on occasional first name terms with the good and the great like Denis Compton and Alex Bedser, (what a handshake *he* had). But, to return to Foulball—sorry, Football, have you noticed the players' boots nowadays? They dazzle like Joseph's coat of divers colours: pink, yellow, green, red, striped and domino-dotted. Yet it only seems a short time ago that boots were, so to speak, boot coloured. Of course, much of this over-decoration is money oriented. Look for instance at Formula 1 drivers, their outfits—and cars—positively covered with labels for almost any product you can think of. Good luck to them (though I think that F1 is an unacceptable waste of resources and a major source of pollution. It's one of the "sports" I would abolish along with boxing and bullfighting).

I hope that our young team will do better than I expect, but to The World Cup? Too much information.

26

My lifetime has been scarred by fearful killings: The Holocaust, that unforgivable industrialised slaughter which included nearly all of my own Dutch relatives. Rwanda with its millions of Hutus and Tutsis. Pol Pot who ruthlessly murdered his educated citizens. There was a TV programme I saw where two not very large African tribes existed with the sole purpose of exterminating the other. No apparent reason. And there are numerous other examples.

Yet, around this universal bloodbath, one quite small example refuses to leave my mind. It was brought back recently when I saw (again) the film *Downfall* which described the last days of Hitler in Berlin. The dreadful crime shown was the deliberate killing of the six children of Josef Goebbels by their mother. First the sleeping draught—forced down the protesting eldest girl and then the young sleepers' teeth crunched down on the cyanide tablet. This seemed to me a crime of such selfishness, such unjustified vanity that I couldn't grasp how apparently human beings could carry it out. Of course, the perpetrators killed themselves too. How could they live with what they had done? And why won't the memory pass me by?

27

Lately there has been a good deal of debate in the papers as to the best age for women to have children. It has particular relevance for me because Zena had our first child at 40 and the second at 43, which, in those days (the 1950s) was considered unusual and risky. Even more so in our case, since Zena had undergone four miscarriages. Thus, our morale had slumped and we already had a private adoption lined up. Also—and I here firmly resist Too Much Information, we had taken measures to avoid further disappointment. Our first son, Richard, used to run half marathons and nowadays, in what used to be called middle age, swims over a thousand miles a year, his yearly quota totalling over sixty *thousand* laps of the large pools he daily frequents. I've often thought—bearing in mind the measures I mention above—that it must have been one super sperm that battled its way to existence.

Still, enough (more than enough I suspect he would say) about Richard, since what I intend to suggest is, taking Zena as an example, that a mature mum can be hard to beat.

Right from the start, Zena rarely put a foot wrong. I remember how she used to read (and of course to Peter, our second) to them at a very early age. There was *Blackberry Farm* where "Joe Robin would be pleased" about the work of the day. There was Walter de la Mare's *Child's Garden of Verse*. "Oh I do like to go up in a swing" ("a fwing" one or other would chip in). "Oh, I do think it's the pleasantest thing / that ever a child can do". So she initiated the love of reading and writing which has characterised their lives. And she was so inventive. When they had colds, she would go up to their bedside with a "nice nice"—a hot drink of lemon and honey—and possibly a very small tot of something to soothe and induce sleep.

Zena had graduated from the University of British Columbia and was extremely intelligent. She was much involved with the boys' learning from an early age and participated in homework, generally encouraged and rejoiced in good results and reports; something which she—and I—tried not to take for granted. In those days, the neighbours in our street consisted not only of Brits (ex-service) but included a splendidly mixed bag of Dutch, Danes, Swedes, Norwegians, French, Welsh and a temperamental Russian, all of whom had children. Zena specialised in making chocolate chip cookies and brownies soon to become almost legendary and a magnet for the children who usually filled our house. In those days, doors were open day and night in the summer, and you were never quite sure which child was where. The great thing was: you didn't need to worry.

I suppose that Christmas was the time when Zena excelled herself. Nothing was missing. With the boys, she dressed the tree ensuring its quota of chocolate ornaments. On Christmas Eve, stockings were stuffed with interesting shapes and surprises, always including a tangerine. (They soon twigged who delivered the stockings; and eventually unmasked the intruder.)

In a houseful of males, sport on the telly loomed large. Much credit then to this apparently elderly Canadian mum, who soon mastered the ins and outs of all the ball games, including esoteric test match cricket. How thrilled she was, watching TV one Sunday afternoon to hear John Arlott describe our spectator sons caught by the TV camera, in complimentary terms. And how loudly she implored our rugger players to bring down (any method approved) the attacking players of the five (later six) nations. And how she glowed watching Pete make 132 not out for his club one Sunday.

What I've been trying to convey is how totally involved Zena was in the lives of the two sons which were the high point of her life.

I think it's fair to say that if you can get everything else right, as she did, bearing a child as the years advance has many positive aspects as well as the few obvious downsides. My sons—and I—struck lucky with what I called my "unique Canadian".

28

Because I'm very deaf in one ear I often use the subtitles when I'm watching TV. Perhaps I'm stating the obvious, but they seem to act more as a hearing aid—something I know must be true because often words which are incorrect on the screen I can hear correctly through the sound. On the other hand, and here I seem to be contradicting myself, I find that the lack of subtitles particularly on, for example, American films, frequently make it almost impossible to follow the dialogue and consequently to understand the plot. Luckily I still have one good ear (spared perhaps after years of artillery activity—both hostile and friendly).

Pencil sketch of author by Helen McLean, 1961.

However, I've often thought how difficult it must be for people who are completely deaf and totally dependent on subtitles. These are, I gather, machine based phonetic translations which produce some hilariously incorrect results. But if you were one of the totally dependent unfortunates, what would you make of "defibrillator" which was titled "different beer later" or "Champs Elysées" with the revised version "chum settling"? Daily, I give thanks for my one good ear which is cherished and no longer allowed to go on aeroplanes.

29

"What's in a name?" cried Juliet. Well, I'll tell you Miss Capulet, there was a great deal in a name for me when I heard it on TV last week as the Tour swept through Yorkshire. Blubberhouses, that was the name; and back I went, back 73 years to Ilkley Moor. Winter 1941 and a couple of dozen of us sit in class, in battledress and forage cap (very rudely nicknamed) with the white strip identifying the wearer as an officer cadet. We were undergoing something called a TEWT, a Tactical Exercise without Troops. One of the Majors on the directing staff has just announced that "a large enemy armoured column is approaching Blubberhouses" and it will be our responsibility (to be replicated at least once in my own later experience) to deter, indeed to destroy these fearsome panzers and their grenadiers. I remember, even then, the apparent incongruity of the name and the scenario, but of course it was inevitable in the circumstances. Ilkley, where my OCTU was located, was reputed to have the best fish and chips in England; something which I never had reason to doubt as I indulged in cod and chips for sixpence in old money, succulent in its daily paper with lashings of salt and vinegar, 2½p! Not everything has improved has it? Blubberhouses .... I suppose you could say it is my Adlestrop.

30

There came a point, one winter I think, where I found the daily walk on Wimbledon Common which I'd shared for so many years with Zena, a bit too testing. So I adopted a circuit of about half a mile from home. It takes me through a little alley bordered on either side by the lush playing fields of KCS, our local public (day) school, then along the south side of the Common, past the two pubs just off the green and back via Ridgway our local "main road". There are occasional unexpected treats. Today, for example, I found a shining black Ferrari convertible. The owner had left the roof open—something I suggest that he could not have done in many places in London. Thus I was able to crane over the side and examine with awe the impressive instruments (no sign of a gear change except maybe two little plaques in the steering wheel). Also, the beautiful leather cream upholstery bordered in black and carrying a stylish "F". Yet when I looked in the back, it became clear that it would only accommodate two very small children. This thunderous monster was, in effect, a two-seater: Wow. Talking of wonderful cars, today's paper carries a story of someone (well-known but who shall remain anonymous) whose husband wishes to build a large underground garage at his Chelsea home to accommodate his "fleet" of cars which include a £350,000 Lamborghini and a couple of Rolls Royce Celestials each valued at £250,000. What's the point? How many can you drive? Looking at my modest Clio, I feel no envy.

Recently, during Martyrdom (Wimbledon Tennis fortnight) these roads were no-parking zones from 8.30 a.m. to *11.30 p.m.* Not a car in sight, yet any other time, so many cars are parked that you'd be hard-put to walk between them.

Something I've noticed during my daily walk is how, when I use the crossing near my home, the weekday drivers (including buses and lorries) always stop to let me cross the road. I wait, leaning on the stick I now usually use. I use my free hand to give obsequious thanks to the drivers on both sides of the road. At the weekend, however, you can't take crossing for granted. Saloons are apt to whizz by as you stand at the stripy edge. Be warned!!

I do quite miss my walk on the Common with the open sky, the golfers, the riders, and the chance to recite swathes of poetry recalled from my youth. I guess some people think that the old gent declaiming "Tomorrow and tomorrow and tomorrow" etc. is a nutcase. And who's to say they're wrong?

31

One day recently, I went shopping as usual. (Tesco, so it must have been Thursday.) It was rather warm and sticky, getting on for 80 as I still prefer to think of it rather than 27 Celsius as those weather people describe it in that dreadfully chatty manner. Anyway, when I reached home with two rather heavy bags of food, I could only just get them in to the house before I slumped in an armchair; and had to spend most of the rest of day lying on my bed. It occurred to me as I lay there, that seventy one years earlier, almost to the day, I had been at war in Sicily in a shade temperature of 118 or about 47 Celsius if you prefer it; not that there *was* much shade. Sometimes we strung camouflage nets over the gun pits to help the gunners, stripped to the waist, sweating as they served their twenty-five pounders. It was probably hotter in the desert which we had just left, but that heat was dry. So dry, in fact, that a cut or graze was almost impossible to heal. Also—and this strikes me so forcibly—when I see young people with bottles of water wherever they go, I'm reminded that in the desert we survived on one enamel mug of tea in the morning and one later in the day.

As a matter of mild interest, I often scan the world temperatures in *The Telegraph* each day. I have discovered that three places which tend to be hottest are Baghdad, Dubai and Riyadh in Saudi Arabia. Riyadh is a place where I believe I had the most frightening moment of my life. It came about that I had stopped there briefly on my way home from, I suppose, the Far East. As we left our aircraft (pre-jet—probably a Super Constellation) I noticed quite nearby, a local, nearly naked, citizen sitting on the wing of an aircraft apparently filling the fuel tank as he, and it shimmered in the fearful heat. From his mouth, dangled a lighted cigarette. Paralysed, I waited for the apocalyptic explosion. For some amazing reason it didn't occur and I reached the relative safety of the airport transit lounge.

I remember one or two other hot spots. In Khartoum you could literally fry an egg on the pavement and Aden and Manila in the Philippines were so humid that it was impossible to dry after taking a shower.

32

Headline in today's *Times* (sent to me in error) "Thousands die as heatwave hits elderly". I have to say that following my experience described above, I wasn't all that surprised. I remember, earlier in life, reading headlines like that which usually accompanied our comparatively rare spells of very hot weather. However, I have to admit that until now they had lacked a certain reality. I suppose they only do when you yourself have become "elderly". I have been lying on my bed, quite unable to get up and do anything. Can this be the person who clambered up Djebel Garci in Tunisia in the "thunder, lightning and rain"—and enemy shellfire; and lived to strike back and kill? Ah, but that was seven decades back. Now, I regard this enfeebled old body and am reminded of Prufrock .... "They will say 'How his hair is growing thin!'" and as I take my daily walk in a short sleeved cotton shirt, "They will say 'But how his arms and legs are thin!'"

Yes, this warm summer is teaching me what I only thought I knew before: what it is to be "elderly", to be so exhausted doing so little and yet unable to do anything more.

33

After that rather pessimistic (not to say self-pitying) piece, the weather has become rather cooler and I've been able to resume my daily walk—though, prudently, early or late in the day. And, I do know that, compared with my few contemporary friends, I am lucky: *able* to walk, *able* to drive, *able* to be in my own home and independent. How I *don't* want to be sitting in a care home where the large muted TV plays to an assorted group of open-mouthed sleepers or blank uncomprehending faces. Again, like Prufrock "I have seen the moment of my greatness flicker / And I have seen the eternal Footman take my coat, and snicker / And in short, I was afraid".

34

Maybe it's just the TV world, but something I've noticed for a long time now is how speakers seem unable to discuss anything without gesticulating. I don't just mean stabbing the air or pointing to emphasise a statement. Many people seem to join their fingers as it were in prayer, to conduct imaginary orchestras or choirs—arms sweeping to and fro, fingers flexing, twitching. The funny thing is that when I was growing up, use of your hands while speaking was considered vulgar—the sort of thing (I seem to remember) that people said was done by Jews, and, by inference, therefore, to be avoided. It was a sort of casual anti-Semitic attitude of the thirties; but not applicable of course to Oswald Moseley or mad Adolf with the incessant waving arms!

35

I was looking in the paper at the picture of some beautiful young actress—can't remember who—laughingly displaying in her wide open mouth a set of wonderful white regular teeth. It reminded me of three things I would love to have had in my life. First, teeth like hers …. to bite into an apple, to chew a juicy steak. Next, to have learned to pilot my own aeroplane. And finally to have been an international concert pianist. All of which have of course, been fantasies never remotely within the bounds of possibility. But harmless enough.

36

Oh dear, after a few blissful soccer-free weeks following our all-too-predictable exit from the World Cup, the football season is upon us once again.

As I've mentioned elsewhere, I myself was a follower (of Arsenal) in the thirties. Many an afternoon have I stood on the Highbury Terrace baying allegiance to those great players: "Boy" Bastin, Ted Drake (*seven* goals in one match) and Denis Compton in the forward line and that stout defence Wilf Copping, Crayston and "Policeman" Roberts.

But—and I claim no originality in this—the game has been ruined by money. Players who are paid each week sums which would be almost laughable if they were not so disgusting. There are young boys in quite modest teams, who are taking home thousands every week; and the top players won't transfer to a club which won't pay them 150,000 a *week*. Also—and this seems an increasing trend—there are now particularly unlikeable managers, with aggressive and manipulative attitudes. I have to admit that most of the criticism above applies to the foreigners who now dominate our "Premier" League, of which we are apparently so proud. It's just rather a pity that it doesn't feature many players from our own country. Hence the unachieving national team. Makes me a bit—not very—sad.

37

It does seem (for reasons which are not obvious to me) that the most ingenious—and prolific—fraudsters seem to operate from Nigeria and Hong Kong. From the latter I have just received the news that, with some small help from me, a huge sum of money will be at my disposal. This is, in fact, the second such missive to come my way; each with a similar theme modified only in detail. I suspect that the same writer is involved. Anyway, this latest effort from Mr James Wei, purports to advise me that someone with my surname, "Arthur Swaab" had, together with Mr Wei, amassed the tidy sum of over 12 million US dollars. Poor Arthur had been "involved in a fatal accident in Mainland China" and—carelessly—intestate, allowed this money to be at the disposal of Mr Wei who generously would identify me as next of kin and proposed to split it with me 50/50 "with no risk to you at all". He urges me to act swiftly, guarantees "100 per cent success" and ends by asking "do not betray my confidence".

I am actually rather a gullible individual. (Last year I was very nearly parted from a sizeable sum; saved only by my bank teller who fetched the police and saved my bacon.) Yet even I could see the absurdity of Mr Wei's proposal—specially the unfortunate (and uncheckable) demise of poor "Arthur". I do find that I almost admire the mixture of sheer naiveté and effrontery of this latest effort (I haven't bothered you with the financial details which were included).

My apparent benefactor includes one email address and ends "I await your response". It'll be a long wait, Mr Wei.

38

Although most of us live in an uncertain world, politicians interviewed (e.g. on TV) don't seem to share our doubts. "I've always been clear on this" says one. "We've always made our policy very clear" declaims another. And sometimes, just to make sure we're convinced, we're told that "I want to be absolutely clear about this".

Maybe it's just me, but all this clarity seems to have passed me by. For example I still don't exactly understand whether membership of the EU is good or bad for our country. So, either I'm a bit dim or things haven't been all that clear after all.

39

One of the wonders of my wonderful, Pete-located Apple computer is YouTube. It enables me to summon all sorts of "temps perdus" from the past. Just lately, courtesy of some famous old-timers on their rather scratchy black label HMV vinyls I have been enjoying Kashmiri song and other Indian love lyrics by Amy Woodforde Finden. I hear my mother (the last one to admit such a thing) trilling herself dramatically as "less than the dust" and the final plaintive cadences of "Pale Hands I loved beside the Shalimar. Where are you now, where ah-ah-ah you now?"

Where indeed? I seem to see the drawing room at Andros, my childhood home. In one corner the Bechstein piano played by my mother and my sister Elly. (And, apparently, given away after the war to some indigent but worthy refugee.) Everything sits on a huge black and purple patterned carpet: on one wall a beaded Ormulu side board with a curved cupboard at each end. There's a sofa, armchairs and small upright chairs. One of these came to me later at some point from Ma's flat and I gave it to Richard along with the desk chair from my bedroom. There is an elegant bow-fronted display cabinet, now cherished by my niece Monica. Her mother, my sister Bé, must have reserved it when Andros was emptied after the war. A glass-topped table contains all sorts of curios. On top of it stands a marble leopard—or possibly some other large cat. I loved that thing, but of course I was still in Germany when Andros and its contents (including mine!) were handed to the tender mercies of Harrods. I remember some pictures of cows grazing in very green countryside. They had large gilt frames but were, as far as I know, not of any great value.

There was a picture of my mother's very handsome parents, which I would give much to own now, but alas, it seem to have disappeared along with the grandfather clock and a home full of furniture and memory-laden odds and ends.

40

After nine months and two days of assiduous courtship, Mina, my lady tabby cat has consented to sleep with me. Mina is my third lady tabby. The first entered my life in 2003. A friend of Richard's told him that a little cat was hiding in her garden, or in the garden shed. Would he be interested in taking what seemed to be a stray? I was quite definite that I would not.

So a few Sundays later we were on our way to Bethnal Green. No definite commitment, mind. Just to inspect. The small cat did the cat things, leg rubbing etc. and was soon in my cat basket homeward bound. On the way, we stopped at Richard's house and let her out while we had a coffee. She then disappeared. We searched the very large house from top to bottom but could find no trace of her. Eventually, in the basement, we found she had hidden under the stairs. I got her home where a dish of Whiskas awaited. I called the little cat Bella and next day took her to the vet. We had been told that Bella was quite young—maybe one or two—but she turned out to be at least nine or ten; and had no teeth—though ate quite vigorously. Later, we discovered that Bella had lived with an old lady who died. The funeral over, the relatives had simply departed and abandoned her. After her three weeks crouched by the microwave, I let Bella out. She had no problem with the cat flap, loved the garden, particularly on summer evenings and was the most loving cat to have shared my life. She liked best to lie full length on me as I lay on my bed reading or watching TV. "He maketh me to lie down in green pastures" I would call out, and in moments she joined me. Bella was probably eighteen when all the fatal signs started to appear and she was laid low by a cancerous tumour. A day came when she limped painfully across the living room floor and let out a small cry. I was unable to speak when I took home from the vet the empty cat basket. Two cats later, I still often think of my first tabby lady.

I grieved greatly for Bella and had no intention of getting another cat. Richard, however, had other ideas. "You are happier when you have a cat living with you, aren't you?" he enquired; and I had to admit that this was indeed the case.

He then drew my attention to the computer website of the Mayhew Animal Home from where he had selected his last cat, Jack. When I looked at "cats waiting to be homed" I was enchanted by tabby Rainbow with her beautiful face and snowy chest. We went to see her and as I rubbed her head and spoke soothing words, I knew she was the cat for me. Mind you, I had to fill in an enormous form and pass a home inspection visit to check that I was acceptable. Rainbow was a young—three or four—vigorous cat, a stray that had evidently lived by her wits, had produced a litter of kittens, and was a considerable hunter. The first time I let her out, she flew lightly over the fence and disappeared for an hour which worried me, but she returned safely.

With all my cats, I tapped on their food bowl as soon as I fed them and this acted as a call home. Rainbow wandered far and as I stood tapping at the gate, I could see her galloping home from down the road. She regularly brought dead birds and mice into the house, usually gobbling them leaving only the tail.

Rainbow never would sleep on my bed but on "Zena's chair" in the living room. I would always go down to say goodnight. She used to roll on to her back but rubbing her chest or belly was too risky as some early lacerations soon convinced me.

Family opinion varies but I have always thought that Rainbow was my most beautiful cat. I still seem to see her stretched out in the sun on the chest of drawers under my bedroom window.

One Saturday morning the phone rang. It was Tim, my vet: "I'm afraid I have very bad news for you." Rainbow's body had been brought in after she had been run over crossing the Ridgway—a hazard for humans let alone cats. Being chipped by the Mayhew, she was readily identified. Deprived once again of my fleet footed feline, I shed a tear and resolved that there would not be another furry companion in my life.

How is it then that I've started this chapter with another lady tabby? Once again, I have to thank / blame Richard who, with casual cunning, drew me reluctantly once more to the Mayhew and its cats which needed a home.

Three year old Mina, my Christmas present from Richard, is a strong-minded little outdoor-loving cat, but she now spends more time with me during the day as well as providing that reassuringly warm lump beside me in the night. Because I'm very deaf in one ear, I have to put the other one close to her to hear her purr. Her purr is not loud, so sometimes I have to rely on her vibrating as—like Bella—she lies stretched out on me. Yes, I suppose I have become a slave to her (as to my other cats), but, as it says in the Book of Common Prayer "In thy service is perfect freedom". I reckon Archbishop Cranmer must have lived with a cat.

41

Early in September, the boys and I spent a weekend in Cornwall. I suppose I must have visited Cornwall nearly a hundred times since the nineteen thirties, but I've never seen it looking better. It was sunny, the breeze was warm and the blue sea, fringed with white foam, made for a sort of Caribbean ambiance. Our one-time landlord, and later friend, John Robinson decided to live at Pilots, the holiday rent described in my last book, and has transformed the house and garden into something you might find in those island paradises inhabited by billionaires. Mind you (as I told him) we still loved it relatively primitive and messy; a place where our bare feet left a sandy floor after a bathe, and the ancient water system tended to boil over at midnight. The countryside looked unusually green this year. I suppose it was the very wet spring but at times it seemed more like motoring through Surrey than the West Country. One afternoon we took the ferry from Padstow to Rock. I remember that Zena and I did that years ago when there wasn't much more to Rock than a fine stretch of sandy beach. Now there are boutique shops and cafés. At one we had a bowl of chips and a soft drink along with the numerous late holidaymakers. Of course, Rock has acquired an unsavoury reputation these days because of the drug-and-booze-fuelled summer activities of wealthy teenagers. There's something special about being on the water even for a short crossing, and that afternoon the sun sparkled on the estuary and the air was wonderfully clean.

There seemed to be many more turbines than last time we came; most of them motionless or turning very slowly. This seemed to back up the claim so cogently argued by Christopher Booker, claiming that these turbines were failing to provide—and would continue to fail to provide—their percentage share of the power required to keep our lights on over the next

Outside 'Pilots', Porthcothan Bay, September 2014. *Left to right*: Pete, Jack, Carolyn Robinson, John Robinson, and Richard.

decades. Certainly the very coldest and frostiest weather is usually not windy. And that's just when the turbines need to be turning briskly round (killing birds and bats their opponents claim). I suppose that *en masse* they do rather ruin the landscape but, individually, I find them rather beautiful.

42

The other day, a commercial droned from the TV with the lugubrious sound of *Wonderful World*, made famous, I suppose, by Louis Armstrong. I think that it's always aggravated me because of a certain wilful optimism which flies in the face of the facts.

"Trees of Green" he crones. But what about Dutch elm disease? And Ash dieback? Not to mention the huge swatches of rain forest—the lungs of the world—being destroyed each year to plant profit-making crops of one kind or another. I've no particular grouch with "Red Roses" which comes next even if they are an excuse for grossly overpricing on 14th February.

But "Skies of Blue" are something else again. Skies in which abundant satellites spy on everyone and everything, reading car number plates for instance from sixteen thousand feet. And what about the increasing number of drones, again spying on us all; or in some cases, killing with pin-point accuracy. Of course it depends where you live but the Bright Day and the Dark Sacred Nights carry their own deadly peril for many.

And the Friends shaking hands are almost certainly outnumbered by the Foes shaking fists. "I love you" they say; but more of them say "I hate you". (Because, when you come down to it, that is what their man-made religions have taught them.) "Babies cry, watch them grow". No, watch them die for lack of a cup of clean water. Watch their famine-swollen bellies and fly-ridden faces.

Alas, there are too many evil people who may one day loose nuclear weapons, on the world blotting out the sun, starving the survivors. The commercial comes to an end. I sing, along with Louis, "I say to myself what a HORRIBLE world". I know I'm very old and very grumpy but "wonderful"?

43

Yesterday evening my ceiling light expired. I know the boys don't like me to replace things like that and truth be told I'm now a bit nervous and unsteady myself. So this afternoon .... a call to Chris my IT wizard neighbour who came in and replaced the bulb in about two minutes. I thought to myself: not long ago I'd have felt mildly humiliated by my inability. However, today there was a certain acceptance of what, I suppose, is Old Age. I was indeed musing that when I was Chris's age, I'd already—long ago—served nearly seven fairly rigorous years in the army. I think that must be what the psalmist had in mind when he wrote that "old men shall dream dreams".

44

For an old person, I sleep reasonably well, though in segments of one and a half to two and a half hours. Often, therefore, in the small hours, I find myself checking the time on the glowing figures of my clock radio. The numbers I see often remind me of things or times past.

1.27 for example was the number of the field regiment I joined at the end of 1942. I'd been in two other regiments in the UK, but, drafted to the Middle East, managed to wangle a posting to a battery commanded by one of my superiors in England for whom I had felt great admiration.

I joined 127 at El Agheila in Libya in what was described as the worst sandstorm they'd ever encountered. It left your eyes very sore for days afterwards. The desert grew very cold at night. I still remember the vivid stars and the sound of the sea on our right flank. I ended up as adjutant of the regiment with whom I served until I was demobilised in May 1946.

2.18 was the phone number of Richard's godmother, Hylda. She lived in Layer de la Haye, an Essex village and was a friend of Clare, my wartime lover. Hylda and her husband Donald were sweet-natured, simple sort of people. He had made a lot of money building wooden boats which were much used on the Nile or some such faraway waterway. They had a big house called Nightingale Corner. It became clear to me why, as I'll explain later. After the war, something caused the boat business to collapse and they lost a good deal. Hylda became an expert daffodil breeder and used to show at the RHS exhibitions. She and Donald sometimes stayed with us on those occasions, the last time, according to our visitors' book was on 3 May 1975; forty long years ago next year. Their son Nicholas was one of my godchildren. I don't think life worked out very well for him and we lost touch which doesn't say much for me as a godfather.

2.24 Clare used to answer her phone "Layer 224". She lived a few minutes up the hill from Nightingale Corner and I used to spend my leave there (and she came up to town with me).

She had a delightful old cottage called Reves, next to the large house owned by her parents.

Clare had chickens which meant eating eggs, a real luxury in 1944 and 45; and she grew asparagus—gloriously fresh and tasty. There were apples which I helped her to wrap in newspaper and store in the barn for the winter. And, yes, the nightingales. I recalled in a diary entry in France in August 1944, how we had stood under a tree in the garden and heard a nightingale sing and sing quite nearby.

Clare and I parted after the war, but were reunited after forty years apart. I went back to Reves from time to time and I remember the huge logs and railway sleepers we piled in the enormous fireplace in the drawing room. Richard and I used to spend a day with her (before she moved to Rutland) and enjoy the Dover soles we bought in Mersea which she cooked for us—swimming in butter and lemon sauce. My favourite food.

Clare and I still speak at least once a week on the phone, reliving the dramatic events we shared in those past days recorded in my first book, *Field of Fire*.

2.25 After war was declared, my parents donated Andros, our family home, for Belgian refugees, and moved to a flat in Chelsea: 225 Nell Gwynn House. I was on leave one day and looked out of one of the windows to see a V1 or buzz bomb or doodlebug as we called them, tootling across the sky nearby. Suddenly, it stopped—as they did—and plunged earthwards where it exploded with a considerable 1,000 lb bang. It was on a later leave (no, I had just been demobbed) that at Reves I received a phone call from my mother at about three a.m. "Your father's *dying*" she wailed. I drove swiftly back through empty city streets, not observing traffic lights too scrupulously. Ma was right. I sat beside Dad's bed as his breathing grew more laboured and he died. He was only 66 and nowadays would have been saved by routine by-pass surgery. I hadn't met Zena then, but two years later, we held our modest wedding reception in the ballroom of Nell Gwynn House. Food was scarce and rationed in those days and the high spot on the menu was an enormous tinned ham (made into sandwiches) sent by my sister Elly from New York. I look at the food ads on the telly this afternoon, and sigh ....

5.04 There was a particularly sickly little song in (I think) the late thirties. I can't remember much about it, but my impression at this great distance, is that a young couple had been up to what a certain broadcaster used to call "A bit of ladies and gentlemen" in Room 504. I suppose I could look it up but I didn't like the wishy-washy thing, and I've only included it because it has reminded me of other wartime songs which I often sing (to myself!) from time to time. Nowadays these songs are regarded as a bit sentimental; and in a way they are. Perhaps we *were* a bit sentimental in those days but facing an uncertain future (death or dismemberment) one clung as it were, to the softer side of life. I remember how, after an all-too-short leave, one would listen to "I haven't said thanks for that lovely weekend". (Those three days in heaven you helped me to spend.)

Another heartfelt song was *There'll be the bluebirds over / the white cliffs of Dover* (And Johnny will go to sleep in his own little bed again). I don't think we knew exactly which birds they were, but we certainly knew they weren't the wings of the Luftwaffe. (My first posting was in Dover where, in 1940, we prepared to repel the mighty Wehrmacht with our ancient, 1917, howitzers; and five rounds per gun.)

Then there was *We'll meet again* (Don't know where, don't know when—that was the point), made famous by Vera Lynn, the Forces Sweetheart. I saw her on TV at some memorial service (last year was it?) and they played a recording of the still rather sweet little ballad.

Another song I remember well (and I think it still gets an occasional airing) is *A nightingale sang in Berkeley Square* first recorded, I believe, by Judy Campbell. The words, still piquant, still retain a certain charm ... "there were angels dining at the Ritz", "The streets of town were paved with stars".

Then there was *Night and Day* with lyrics, I think, by Cole Porter. I remember getting a letter in the Libyan desert from a person who made memorable for me, a short stay in Cairo. "Night and day", she wrote "You are the one". Hard to reconcile my young—and presumably engaging—self then with the rather crumbling noneagarian of today.

And, let me not forget, what was probably the best song of the war: the German *Lili Marlene*. We of the Eighth Army first heard it from the Africa

Korps on desert nights and quickly took it up, perhaps on the Salvation Army's principle: why should the Devil have the best tunes? I think that Lale Andersen who first gave us Lili, also recorded an English version which I recall to this day .... *Underneath the lantern / by the barrack gate / Darling, I remember / the way you used to wait.* Marlene Dietrich also recorded Lili as did our own Vera Lynn.

5.55 Advertised before the war as "the best cigarette in the world" State Express 555 was one of the cigarette brands I advertised twenty years later. I was able to do so with conviction as my father used to give me a pre-war Christmas present of 100 Three Fives (in little yellow tins which still hold screws, nails, rawlplugs and other oddiments in my toolbox). When cigarette advertising was banned from TV, my campaign for Three Fives was singled out as exemplifying all the evils of cigarette promotion. An unintended accolade, perhaps.

7.32 It's a summer morning, term is over and I'm strolling along Radipole Road towards Weymouth station. The train to London starts at 7.32 and reaches Waterloo at 11.08. Some other Londoners and others are with me. We have cast aside those school uniforms including our straw boaters (which we called Bashers); by today's standards, however, we are still pretty formal: sports jackets, a tie and grey flannels. I can still recall the insouciance, the almost literal smell of freedom on the seaside air as one visualised the long summer holiday ahead, possibly somewhere exciting abroad but so desirable wherever it turned out to be. The streets were almost empty which seemed in some way to add to the pleasure of it all. Once on the train, we all light up our (unfiltered) cigarettes—probably Players, 5p for twenty. Almost imperceptibly the landscape begins to slide away. We hear our noble locomotive: chomp .... chomp ....chompchomp. Smoke drifts past the windows, we pick up speed. The holiday begins. Yes, Wordsworth, "to be young was very heaven".

45

Step forward, Jack Swaab, a.k.a. Townmouse J, and forgetful old fool. Banging on all that time about numbers and omitting one of the most significant of all: 3:03. Yes, the A303, that history-laden road to the West

Country, on which you've spent so many hours of your life; starting, I suppose, in the summer of 1954. Zena and I (recently cured of TB) set out in our heavily laden, but game A40—the "ah ho" one sunny morning heading for St Minver in Cornwall, where we had booked in at a farmhouse. In those days it was a rare luxury to find even a small stretch of dual carriageway and I remember that it took us four hours to reach Wincanton.

A bit further westwards we passed some people with their head in the bonnet of our twin A40. I was filled with enough HK milk in those days—Human Kindness—to stop and ask if I could help. Their problem was the starter motor. Now, it so happened that I had had similar (probably endemic to A40) trouble with my starter motor and—with the aid of my local garage—had devised a way to fix it from inside the bonnet. "This is what you press" I was able to advise our fellow travellers; and sure enough, the engine burst into life. Grateful cries echoed in our ears as we pushed on westwards, joining the A30 towards Honiton (then a narrow, congested road) and then deep into wild, deserted Cornwall.

However, coincidence had a further surprise for us for who should be staying at that very farmhouse in St Minver but our stranded A40 friends. I can't remember whether they were four people or just the two, Pat and Norman Codd whom I've located in an ancient address book with their names more or less crossed out. They lived in Reigate and we remained on Christmas card terms for some years, but whether we met again I can't recall.

Most of the people, though not all, in that address book are dead now. (I'll resist expressing the obvious thought which crosses my mind.)

Very different these days are my forays on the A303. My destination now is the School of Royal Artillery at Larkhill on Salisbury Plain where, if I survive, I'm to lecture for the eighth time to the Young Officers' group. (The background to this is in my last book, *Slouching in the Undergrowth*.) But very different, too, because I'm driven down there in my own car by Pete who also reads extracts from my first book for the Y.O.s. Now, of course, we only enter the A303 when we veer off the M3 to the road over which the 303 is signed (as well as on the road itself). Then we come off it, turning right onto A345 after crossing the Avon at the new roundabout.

But the 303 holds many small reminders for me. How in the old days we used to turn left on the Blandford–Warminster road (the A350) to visit our friends the Balkwills at Century Cottage near Shaftesbury. And once we left it to visit The Lamb at Hindon—famous but, as I remember, a bit disappointing.

I can't leave tales of the 303 without mentioning the world heritage site at Stonehenge. Zena had never seen this before and in those days we were able to amble round the stones, touching them with perhaps, some sort of reverence. Nowadays, there is a visitor centre which I certainly wouldn't want to visit, and the stones are fenced off against vandalism. There is now planned a 1.8 mile tunnel off the A303 because of the (undisputed) traffic congestion along a single carriage road. I can understand this, but am glad that I have many times seen this iconic monument looming out of the mist as you swoop down towards that long (narrow!) stretch to Winterbourne Stoke. Wouldn't want to live there. (But always thought what fun it would be to move to Grately (now off the M3) and call your house "Rejoice".)

Nowadays, visiting Cornwall we leave the 303 at A358 which takes you (rather slowly because the road's a bit narrow) past Langport where we have coffee, across to the M5, then down to the A30 onto Cornwall. There used to be a tradition in which the boys would chant Devon, Devon, Devon, Cornwall, Cornwooool as we drove downhill across the county border after Launceston and turned right onto A395 for Camelford and the Cornwallish ambience.

46

A number of the charities whom I've been supporting with small sums of money for quite a few years, have been kind enough to send me address stickers to identify letters I send. I've felt recently that they seemed to be numerous and varied; and on an impulse, counted them: 1176.

At my estimated usage in the near future, I already have enough for another sixteen or seventeen years. Even the most extreme optimism (or, possibly, pessimism), will not see me around in the twenty thirties. I feel I should advise the donors, but don't want to sound ungrateful.

47

Christmas once again. I meander mentally over the increasingly distant years. A couple of tiny memories come to me. I was a very small boy when, one Christmas morning, I woke early to find my stocking, duly complete with mysterious and exciting lumps. There was a torch which shone red, green or white as you slid the switch up and down. And, above all: a WATCH, yes a pocket watch, already telling me the time (can't remember what it was) and in its lower half you could see the mainspring and the little wheel going to and fro. It was my first watch, what a treasure.

I was also a small boy who went down to the kitchen, always so snug with its open fire and big table in the middle. Our cook, Lizzie was there, and her sister Sarah who came as charlady in mid-week. They were singing a carol about "three Kings from Orientar". At least, that's what I thought; and it was rather a disappointment later in life, to discover that Orientar wasn't a country after all.

Then, all those Christmases slightly tarnished by Dad's disastrous attack on the mountainous turkey. The threepenny bits and other silver things in the Christmas pudding and furtive evening visits to the larder to spread dripping on the toast which we had made with long toasting forks over one or other of the open fires. Andros, my home, was heated with open fires, gas fires and large enamel "Esse" stoves, all of which consumed large quantities of anthracite and ordinary, cheaper coal. I remember the horse drawn carts with their loads of coal sacks leaning on one another. The coal men—darkened it seemed by their cargo—used to heave a sack and stagger down the path which ran alongside the house. There they lifted a manhole which led to the cellar and deposited their load. In the house, the roaring noise of the descending coal was like a small thunderstorm.

The Esse stoves burned all night in the winter and had to be re-filled early by Jessie a.k.a. Nag, my old nurse but now housemaid each day. I sometimes thought of that when we were in Cornwall, relighting the little stove in the kitchen. Mervyn used to call it "R and R" for riddling and replenishment.

It was one of Zena's particular gifts to create a Christmas time magic for us all. There was the tree, laden with tinsel, bright baubles and chocolate ornaments (which diminished with mysterious speed). Zena's mince pies (she used to make four or five dozen for us and neighbours) were hugely admired. Her brownies and chocolate cookies became legendary and are recalled by old friends to this day. Later, she used to make Norwegian fridge pudding and ginger "coek" like my mother's (only not *exact* because Ma would never divulge the recipe—even to my sisters).

48

2015

So it's 2015. And the New Year opens with the same litany of death, disaster and disconsolation that marked its predecessor. Twenty-six killed at worship; sixty more by a rocket fired at a wedding party; eight thousand perishing miserably with the ebola virus; 162 hapless individuals plunged with their airplane below the Java Sea.

It always—and pointlessly—fills me with a sort of futile rage as I hear the various prelates (even the new apparently rather sensible Archbishop of Canterbury) assuring us that "God" loves the world and all of us; even as he sent his Tsunami last year and disposed of another quarter of a million of his children. The religious dignitaries all tell us about "God" but nobody defines this being. I watch several of the programmes about the universe (one of many universes) and there soon comes a point where one can't grasp the immensity of everything. But, and equally, it seems obvious (to me, anyway) that "God" as taught by man-made religions is absurd, unbelievable and as Marx (was it?) said: the opiate of the masses. There, I've had my annual grouse and if I survive to another new year—by no means certainly—I'll probably welcome 2016 with another rant.

Meanwhile, with my addiction to significant numbers, I remember that 2015 "twenty fifteen" (14th Avenue West, Vancouver) was the number of Zena's Canadian home. I visited it on one of the several trips I took to Vancouver (thanks to securing the Canadian Pacific Airline account). As Zena's illness progressed, she used to ask me as we went shopping, whether we'd be visiting 2015, or perhaps "Granville and tenth" or "Robson Street".

Yes, with increasing age, weakening mental and physical ability, I do find my general mood is rather sad, though I'm encouraged by the "robust" character I'm given by my sons' friends; and, indeed, my own friends.

49

Last week, I went to visit an old friend in a local care home. This is a very good care home run by some pleasant nuns. At one time—must be forty or fifty years ago I suppose—Zena and I went on their waiting lists. Luckily I found a very helpful place for Zena because I don't think we could have afforded the one I've described; certainly I couldn't now. Anyway on this visit, my friend, who is now unable to walk, was not in a very communicative mood and as he dozed contentedly from time to time, thus not calling for much input from me, I was able to observe the three elderly ladies each in her own armchair. One lay more or less on her side, sleeping, the next dozed intermittently, her chin falling to her chest, and the third stared steadily into space. Their thinning hair showed pale scalps, their arms and legs were boney and their faces colourless and wrinkled. I felt deep pity for those old ladies. I thought how once they'd been small girls leaping with delight on summer days and later, desirable young women with lovers and husbands. Then I thought perhaps I was projecting what might be my own reactions if and when the time might come. We do, perhaps, suffer more than these old people—particularly those with dementia. It may be that within their private world they are wandering perhaps wistfully but without stress as one feels sometimes on the verge of sleep. I used to worry about Zena in this way, because her last years were devoid of real pleasure. And so it was, I felt, with these three old ladies. You couldn't call it living really. More just existing till their frail bodies stopped struggling. Another old friend and I frequently express the hope that we shan't lose our independence and land up in what they call God's waiting room. I plodded home on that cold morning, grateful that (albeit with my stout hospital walking stick) I was still able to do so—even if I felt I had to be especially careful of the wet leaves on the pavement. Yes, a mere shadow of the young fellow who so often faced enemy gunfire. But how many—shadows or not—like me—are still here to grumble?

50

The country has been commemorating the 50th anniversary of Churchill's state funeral. Much has been written about the 300,000+ citizens who queued for hours in the frosty days and nights, the tears that were shed by many in the queues which stretched for up to three miles on both banks of the Thames. Together with a work colleague who had also served in the army, I went on a bitterly cold night and spent four hours, starting on the south side of Lambeth Bridge, for our few seconds in Westminster Hall. The queue was so long that it snaked back along itself and it was impossible to judge when one's turn would come.

I remember how quiet everyone was. You heard footsteps on the pavement and later, the tiny swishing sounds of many feet on the carpeted hall. I still recall the amazement I felt as I entered a place which had seen so much of our history. It seemed grey and rather gloomy, emphasising the brightness of the coffin, draped in the Union Jack, high on its catafalque. On its top lay Winston's Order of the Garter insignia. At each corner, their swords reversed, heads bowed, a guardsman in full regalia, shining in the light of six massive candles. Above the bier stood a tall gold and jewelled cross.

The thing that struck me then, and has remained with me ever since, was the complete silence of so many people as we spent our all-too-short solemn moment in what we recognised as an historical event. Those of us who had served in the war, felt that we were honouring perhaps the greatest Englishman of all time. Zena, with impeccable instinct, took Richard, then aged nine to the lying in state. He has told me that—as for me—it has been something unforgettable in his life. Pictures on the TV this week have brought back the grandeur and emotion of those 50 year old events. Yet, in a way, it was quite simple. We felt that he had saved us; and we were saying thank you.

51

Along with most of the "civilised" world, I have been racked with revulsion triggered by the disgusting cruelty of the so-called Islamic State. (Though Wolf Hall on TV reminds us that Catholics and Protestants have been—like IS—burning each other to death. However, as some sort of excuse, that was about 500 years ago.) However, I have been much more wrung out by a second showing on BBC4 of Shoah (Hebrew for Destruction). The description of the poor women at Treblinka, naked, their bowels emptied in terror. The graphic description of the death struggle in the gas chamber (5 canisters of Zyklon B to kill 3,000 men, women and children), the last named trampled to death, their small skulls broken as the strongest fought for non-existent air. I find it difficult to contemplate, let alone describe this scene. We talk of Hell as some sort of fearful punishment after death but what could be more dreadful than the gas chambers at the death camps.

Yet, for all their barbaric behaviour, the IS do at least fall back on what may (or may not) be a perverted, religiosity based on Allah and his prophet. Nor—unlike the organisers of Shoa—do they degrade their victims even before their deaths; cutting off their hair, pulling out gold teeth, piling up their shoes, their spectacles, their dentures all for industrial use. Even their poor bodies were sometimes rendered down to make soap.

And, of course, before all this, their shops, their houses, their possessions had been stolen and handed to all who supported the Nazi rulers. Oh yes, it was enjoyably profitable for some.

When I hear a bleating parson on Radio 4's Sunday service asking "You" to ease the suffering in the world, I can't resist shouting at the radio. "Ask 'You' what he was doing about suffering in 1942". Pointless, of course. Just one's rage against the inhumanity of humanity; making its reappearance in our own country even as I write.

52

Last week, went to the School of Artillery at Larkhill on Salisbury Plain to give a talk—my eighth—to the Young Officers' course. I've recounted in my last book how I came to be invited by the Commandant in 2008; and how it has become a regular feature of the YO course, prior to their visiting the Normandy battlefields.

The talk has, by now, settled into a pattern: I describe some of my misspent life and military ventures which Pete illustrates with readings and recollections from *Field of Fire* and my second book, *Slouching in the Undergrowth*. We're also lucky enough to be able to entertain them with a

THE ⚜ TIMES

Army calls in WWII veterans to teach recruits about war

Jack Swaab passes on the lessons learnt in six years eight months in uniform   Times photographer, Ben Gurr

Simon de Bruxelles
Last updated at 10:19AM, October 29 2012

The first time Jack Swaab visited Larkhill Barracks on Salisbury Plain it was the 10th of December 1941 and he was a newly-minted second lieutenant.

The date is engraved on his memory not just because it was the first time he heard a big gun fire at close quarters, but because it was the day two of the Royal Navy's mightiest battleships, HMS Prince of Wales and HMS Repulse, were sunk by the Japanese.

Yesterday, he was back at the army's School of Artillery to pass on some of the

Story from *The Times*, first posted 28 September 2012, reporting on Jack Swaab's talk—reporter, Simon de Bruxelles, photographer, Ben Gurr.

The author at Larkhill in September 2012, flanked by staff and some of the trainee young officers.

BBC archive tape I discovered in 2005, recording some rather large bangs from a rather small battle in November 1944 when I hosted a notable war correspondent at my OP in Holland.

Recently I've tried to put my talk into perspective by reminding them that had *I* been addressed by a 96 year old when I was their age, he'd have been describing events such as the Charge of the Light Brigade, the Indian Mutiny and the debacle at Isandlwana.

These were only things in my history book at school, whereas the events I tell them about are mostly recorded on film, radio or TV and, though distant, familiar to them. I much admire these young men and women who have undergone gruelling initial training at Sandhurst before being selected as elite Royal Artillery Officers. I usually conclude by telling them they are likely to perform just as well as, if not better than us, and wish them good luck. They usually respond with quite numerous and intelligent questions so I generally go home feeling that I've left them something of value. I'm encouraged in this belief by letters I've received from the senior officers in charge of the course; from which I (immodestly) quote a few extracts:

'A note to thank you once again for a truly inspiring presentation prior to our Battlefield Study in Normandy'.

'You spoke eloquently about your remarkable experiences not just "at war" but about your life and the various experiences that have made you who you are'.

'Thank you so much for another humorous, intriguing but informative presentation for the Young Officers'.

'It never fails to amaze me how you manage to captivate this young generation with all aspects of your wartime experiences. It also never fails to amaze me how captivated I am both by you in person and by the content of your diaries'.

'It was a real privilege to meet you and Pete and to hear the accounts of your incredible experiences. It was all delivered in such a clear, but humorous manner—it definitely set the standard for the younger generation!'

'Thank you very much indeed for coming to Larkhill to speak to the Gunner recruits and Young Officers about your fascinating experiences seventy years ago. You provided a touch of realism and realisation which enabled the YO's to better appreciate and understand aspects of the Normandy campaign once they were deployed on the ground in Northern France. It was a fascinating trip and I thank you for setting them off on the right foot'.

As we sold one or two books last year, Pete suggested that we take a few more this time and we sold all six *Field of Fire* and a couple of *SITU*. I was happy to sign them.

We've been invited back on the afternoon of 4th May, preceded by lunch as usual in the impressive mess with its huge chandeliers. Not at all like my first visit as a 2nd Lieutenant in December 1941.

53

Yes, it was going to be ONE OF THOSE. I knew it as soon as I drew the curtains. From a grey sky fell the dismal rain. Day had broken with Tennysonian blankness. I seemed to hear the growling of Winston's dog as it rubbed against my legs. This is the kind if mood that hits you—anyway, hits me—in very old age on a day when you realise that you have absolutely nothing you need do; and you won't be seeing another soul before the early winter darkness sets in.

No more sex of course. That disappeared a long time ago. I remember I was taking some tablets (suddenly the name comes back to me; Finasteride) for prostate trouble. On a routine hospital visit a young lady doctor asked me—brightly, just to show how unshockable she was—"Not so many erections then?" "What's an erection?" I grumped.

Sex remains a rueful memory. There was something so unique about the soft warmth of a lover's body ... Where, as the doomed young Canadian soldier wrote "love throbs out in blissful sleep ... And hushed awakenings are dear."

Actually, I think I've stopped fretting about the absence of sexual activity. There came a sort of resigned realisation that it would be rather more trouble than it was worth; rather tiring in fact. Though even committing such a suggestion to paper is an obvious by-product of a bad day—not at the office but, as I said earlier, at the drawn curtain on a rain swept morning.

Poor old Prufrock with his white flannel trousers walking on the beach. I think of him when my sons take me on a welcome Cornish holiday where once I ran eagerly to meet the surf. Now, I pick my way (aided of course by my omnipresent stick) gingerly across the rocks. Still, I continue to enjoy finding a sort of natural rock-bed on which to lie in the sun and watch the af'rug (a new word to me, too) of the waves as they cream their way onto the beach.

Prufrock wondered whether he dared to eat a peach. I've never had that problem. I recall those succulent peaches I used to enjoy in Italy before the war. How the juices spilled uncontrollably down your chin, the smooth sweet yet sharp taste of the slippery round body. And in Sicily in 1943 we used to pick them off the trees as we fought our way slowly north. But I've found supermarket peaches ("ripe and ready to eat") a big no-no. They usually aren't and in most cases are rather dry; and usually end up in the bin. Too much trouble to wait a week to complain.

No, the fruit which spells trouble for me is the dear old reliable apple. It's many years since I could bite a chunk out of my favourite Granny Smith or Cox's Orange Pippin. I watch with sour envy when some young female model chops her white regular teeth into that firm round fruit, extracting a juicy segment.

About the only physical feature I've envied all my life is one of those mouths filled with white, regular teeth, visible right to the back when the owner opens wide to laugh. I've always had rotten teeth—in fact we all had, except Elly who, in the thirties went to live in New York—at that point far ahead of our stone age dentistry. And you're not really trouble-free even when you've got false teeth. Sore gums, dangerous pips etc. I remember a pre-war girlfriend whose teeth were so regular, so white that everyone thought they were false. She married a conscientious objector who farmed in Dorset with a rather well-known poet / playwright.

54

This week's been all about The Budget, though why anyone gets excited I don't know. Pretty well everything is "leaked" in advance and most changes don't affect ordinary people like me. The Budget never *did* mean much to me. I mean I've always just handed out PAYE on anything I've earned plus a bit of interest from bonus savings; and nowadays it comes already taxed. Anyway I listened to George Osborne as he spun his millions, then billions and his decimal points and other percentages and I did feel how completely pointless (no pun intended) it was since nobody could really understand it; a sort of financial emperor's new clothes. It was a very competent performance, enjoyed by the Tory benches, though it's never going to get him the leadership if that's what he wants. It was amusing to watch Nick Clegg—shackled by coalition bonds—sitting blank faced or scowling throughout. And it was depressing that the best Ed Miliband could do was an outburst of class warfare with its misleading stuff about millionaires.

The thought that this rather weird individual might become Prime Minister genuinely frightens me. Better dead than Ed.

55

Melanie, one of his daughters, phoned me to say that Bill French had died on Sunday. He'd been in a local care home on Wednesday for a few days after a week in A&E at St George's, following a fall at home. Nothing broken, but bruises, abrasions and that loss of confidence which comes with 98 hard-lived years. I went to see him on the Thursday and we discussed his plan to spend three weeks getting his strength back to return home—where I'd visited every Wednesday on my way home from Richard's house, for some years. Like the old men we were, we rambled on about our early time together, exactly seventy years ago. He always told me how welcome he'd been made when posted to our (304) battery which he commanded (in which I was a troop commander). I see, looking at *Field of Fire*, my record of those times, that on 1 February 1944 I wrote "Bill French, a 'floating' major from 59 Agra is coming to us. He's a very nice chap—I went with him to that VT fuse lecture the other day". And on 12 February during a lull in a gruelling little battle, I added "Bill French is excellent to work with and has made a very good impression all round". Bill turned out to be a brave, competent soldier. He was mentioned in Dispatches and—something he only told me recently—recommended for a Military Cross, which was refused because he'd not been with the regiment long enough (how absurd).

On Wednesdays we'd share our health worries and problems and our hopes to see out our remaining days independent in our own homes; and spared the prospect of hospital and care home. I know that enfeebled as he was and increasingly beset with failing health—Bill won't have resented his unplanned but not altogether unkind departure. Bill loved his golf and his bridge. He was one of the best players I've enjoyed playing with since 1945 in occupied Germany. Zena and I used to have such enjoyable evenings with him and Nora. I shall miss him.

56

It's Easter again and I've a quite haphazard recall of three past Easters. The first, I think, must have been in 1947 because I was demobbed after Easter 1946 and by 1948 I was married in May and far too busy at Easter for the occasion I have in mind. I had hired a large car—a Humber I think from some firm I can't remember—it was in the days before Hertz and Avis— and I drove six of us to Rye where we stayed at The Mermaid. There were Zena and I, engaged to be married before long, two of Zena's Canadian flatmates: Mary a tall beauty from New York State and Audrey a brunette sexpot. Lastly, John whose family were leading citizens in Sydney; and my best man, Roger who looked very much like the Hollywood actor, Basil Rathbone. John had fallen in love with Mary at one of our previous weekends near Bodiam Castle. They were married a bit before us, I think. I always remember that John's rather aristocratic mother gave Zena and me an intro to the Prideaux-Brune family with their enormous estate in Cornwall. Roger was in hot (and unsuccessful) pursuit of Audrey. He later settled for a less glamorous, very pleasant Canadian heiress. She, Helen, got Parkinson's and died many years ago as did Roger a few years later. I have two old snapshots of that weekend in Rye. One, I must have taken, of my five companions, and one of Zena and I sunbathing in the dunes, I,

In Rye, 1947. *Back row, left to right*: Mary Heyer and Audrey Salter. *Front row, left to right*: John Dowling, Zena, and Roger Andrews.

very skinny in swimming trunks, Zena showing a large amount of shapely thigh.

You know, whenever I think of the Prideaux-Brunes I recall how Mervyn, who was very mischievous cried out on seeing the magnificent sweep of the staircase exclaimed "Isn't that an Opie?" (Having earlier ascertained from a guide book that it certainly was.) "Isn't that an Opie?" became a piss-taker for us both for years. Mervyn also, among other pranks, introduced me to some unsuspecting café owners in rural Portugal as "James Hunt the racing driver". Not for nothing did I describe Mervyn in my speech at his 70th as "a master of the straight-faced lie". My best friend, much missed. I digress. Well, that's how I'm writing this book.

At an earlier Easter (26 April 1943 I discover from Google), I was manning for 24 hours an extremely uncomfortable, and rather dangerous OP on the Djebel Garci, a small mountain in Tunisia. Because it had previously been occupied (and could be seen by the Germans), it had to be occupied and evacuated before first light, as we used to call dawn.

In my diary I recorded how one of some eighty, 105 mm shells blew in part of the OP, with something hitting my tin hat and nearly knocking me out. (Shellfire in mountain terrain was particularly unpleasant as the hard surface encouraged the number and spread of shell splinters; something less threatening in the wet mud of Holland a year later.) I hadn't realised until I was thinking about Easter this week that seventy two years ago my Easter eggs had been so explosive.

The other Easter which remains fixed in my memory dates back to a time—when because the boys were young—we were able to take two holidays each year at wonderful Porthcothan. On one occasion we arrived to see the beach covered with *snow*—never seen—at least, by us—before or since, and I imagine (though I haven't resorted to omniscient Google to find out) an unusual occurrence during the twentieth century.

57

Bill's memorial service today at St Mary's—our rather fine parish church close to the tennis courts, (which enables them to let the church grounds for daily car parking during Martyrdom (cf *Slouching in the Undergrowth*), presumably collecting a great deal of money for the church). It was what I regard as a "comfortable C of E" service; familiar hymns, not unduly pious or too long. Tributes from family including younger brother, son Steven, grandchildren etc. Have just filed his very well produced Order of Service along with nineteen others I have accumulated over my drawn-out years.

58

I suppose it's an aspect of living alone, but over the years I've noticed that I rarely switch off the radio without adding "shut up". Often I say this quite mildly without animosity but occasionally if one of my (numerous) *bêtes noires* is speaking, I bark out the words sharply.

I'm always reminded—not altogether appositely—of the occasion described in Orwell's *1984*. O'Brien, the apparent rebel but actual secret policeman turns off the TV image of Big Brother. This is what follows: "Julia uttered a tiny sound, a sort of squeak of surprise. Winston was too much taken aback to be able to hold his tongue. 'You can turn it off!' he said. 'Yes' said O'Brien 'we can turn it off. We have that privilege'".

So I have my O'Brien moments. (I have quoted from my first edition of *1984*. Lacking a jacket and rather careworn from use over the years, it isn't as valuable as items bought for later sale as opposed to present pleasure.)

59

It was one of those mornings on which Wordsworth said "to be young was very heaven" so I decided to walk—as I used to—on the Common instead of my usual very urban circuit. It was (unsurprisingly) quite hard to find a parking space at the end of Sunset Road, but I squeezed into a shady spot and set out between the trees on to the large open space where I've always recited favourite poems. I didn't today. I think I was concentrating on overcoming the rather weak feeling in my right knee, at present afflicted with arthritis (not improved by the wound inflicted on it by German gunners some seventy years ago).

I saw several dozen golfers in their bright red garments and dust flew from the tracks as the lucky horsemen cantered along. I thought of the smooth power I used to grip between my thighs as I galloped my shiny black horse, Kondor, through the forest on such a sunny morning in Germany seven decades back. Looking to the north I could see the big passenger jets making their approach to Heathrow, the sun glinting on their wings.

Happily, the seat I used to share with Zena was empty. I sat there in the sun remembering days past and the sadness of her last walks and rest on this very bench. The heather where we scattered her ashes on that cold December morning is beginning its springtime growth. The shrub which we christened "Zena's tree" and decorated with a bright red ribbon (which disappeared) has grown so large that I couldn't identify it with confidence among the group of small trees.

I couldn't do the complete walk I used to but plodded back along a shorter route beside the trees. Several dog walkers greeted me. We all agreed that it was a beautiful day.

Wimbledon is a good place to live at this time of year. The streets are lined with pink and white blossom. Like Housman I "see the cherry hung with snow". Even in my own small garden there is a dazzling white camellia. Next to it is a scented viburnum and the courtyard is filled with various undemanding but colourful shrubs.

It is afternoon and the sky remains what Mervyn and I used, rather tipsily, to call "cloudless blue" on those rare Cornish days when it was. It became a sort of code word for unfounded optimism.

60

Now here's a coincidence. A couple of days after I described, in chapter 55, my spell in an OP in Djebel Garci in Tunisia, there was an obituary in *The Telegraph* of Col. Peter Jones who—brave fellow—as a company commander, won an immediate DSO at Enfidaville a few days earlier. He and his Gurkhas wielding their lethal Kukris had a stiff battle with the

Germans which no doubt accounted for the headless corpses heating in the African sunshine around my OP. We'd always understood them to be Italians; but in any case, I didn't hang around to identify them.

I read in this obit that Djebel Garci was over a thousand feet high, bringing back a fading memory of that night scrambling up the mountain in a thunderstorm, lashed by rain—and occasional shellfire. With us plodded our brave mules, laden with our heavier equipment. 1st battalion 9th Gurkha Rifles, the unit which captured this position, was part of the 4th Indian Division, one of that small but memorable band of brothers, the Eighth Army. Their divisional sign was (I think) a red kite, universally referred to as "The Shitehawk". Most of us had nicknames. The 30th Corps was known as "The Pig"—or sometimes something a little more descriptive. My own outfit wore the HD, standing for Highland Division, but always known as Highway Decorators—due perhaps to our insistence on making lavish use of an HD sign as we advanced. Then there was the TT of the excellent 50th Division— the Teetotallers whose sign identified their origin in the north country and the Tyne and Tees rivers. Prominent too, were the original Desert Rats, the 7th Armoured Division with their Jerboa. The media have turned many of us before and since into "Desert Rats" but the true claim to the title must surely rest with the 7th Armoured. Nor could I forget the splendid soldiers of the 2nd New Zealand Division with its silver fern leaf. "Two NZ" were always regarded as good troops to have on your flank. Of course, later on, in Europe, the tight-knit comradeship of the Eighth Army could not be sustained in the much larger invasion force. The jacket of *Men under Fire*, a book in my library, shows twenty Divisional and other signs but, understandably, none achieved the closeness of the Desert Army with its inspirational commander.

61

Last week I went to Larkhill to give my talk to the Young Officers' Group for the ninth time. I've given a good deal of thought to introducing my story because, as I learned as an Ad Man, you need to engage your audience from the beginning. For the first seven occasions I used to recount my first visit to Larkhill as a 2nd Lieutenant on 10 January 1941. I recalled the exact date because it was the one on which two of our battleships were sunk by Japanese bombers off Malaya.

The purpose of that visit was to hear a gun fired for the first time; and describing the single ponderous shot from an ancient howitzer, I contrasted it with a night battle at Mareth two years later when I emerged dazed from the 450 rounds each of our 25 pounders had fired.

Time came when I began to feel that this intro had become a bit stale; or maybe I had just become a bit bored by it. Anyway with Group 8 and Group 9 I asked them to guess at *my* feelings if—at their age—I had been given a talk by a 97 year old. I pointed out that they were able to relate to what I described because it had all become so familiar through the medium of film or TV or wireless. Whereas I, back in 1938, would only have had history books, epic poems or perhaps an occasional play to bring back tales of such events as the Charge of the Light Brigade or how—as a gunner—one might have strapped the bodies of defeated Indian mutineers to gun barrels and blown them to pieces as they shouted "Jai Hind". A Queen, I reminded them, would have been on the throne but it was Queen Victoria. It was only after this, I hoped, diverting contrast, that I continued with December 1941 and my life leading up to that landmark occasion.

I always enjoy talking to the YOs, particularly the girls, the young women, who, to my old fashioned instincts seem strange as soldiers. Yet, when hearing their (arduous) route via Sandhurst to a single pip in the Royal Artillery, I am always impressed by their intelligence, courage and outgoing personalities. My companion at lunch last time had graduated with an English Master's degree from Durham University, and rowed for the Army. (I sometimes feel a bit embarrassed when I come to that part of my talk devoted to life in the Desert Army—"shitting and shaving"— but the young ladies probably take it in their stride more easily than I do myself.)

Pete, who shares my presentation, and I particularly enjoy lunch in the Officers' Mess with its fabulous chandeliers, lit one night while we had dinner, and the east and west dining tables, some seventy feet long. The high table, a mere twenty-six feet, was originally used by the blood-soaked surgeons in the Crimean War, and donated to the mess for a less sanguine usage. The walls are hung with huge portraits of eminent persons past and present, and the regimental silver collection, including various items from parts of the Quondam Empire simply has to be seen to be believed.

(My eighth talk was filmed and put on DVD which is being sent to me. I like to think that in the distant future, gunners may perhaps view this ancient FOO in days when such outdated operators won't be needed.)

62

Something new at Larkhill this time. To mark the 300th anniversary of the founding of the Royal Artillery, the school, its headquarters, is sending a baton around the world to gunners far and wide, starting on this very day on its journey to Australia and New Zealand. Two youngest YOs have handed it over, flanked by an elderly brigadier who also gives a talk to the group, and myself. So we stood in front of an old gun, blinking (I was, anyway) in the sunshine as we were photographed and videoed and the baton started on its long and rather historic journey.

The author and young officers with the Royal Artillery baton at the start of its round-the-world journey.

63

It is the centenary of the execution by the Germans of Nurse Edith Cavell in October 1915. She had stayed in Belgium, where she nursed wounded soldiers of both combatants. She also joined an escape organisation which organised the escape of at least 200 British soldiers; and for this she was condemned to death by firing squad. Hers was one of the first monuments I remember visiting at the north end of Trafalgar Square as a small boy. It is inscribed with "Patriotism is not enough," her own words. I remember being much moved by a film in which—disdaining a blindfold—the noble nurse walked to her death singing the hymn Abide with me. Abide with me. One of the minor aggravations of my life has been the singing of this hymn at the FA Cup Final since 1927. The complexion—both religious and literal—of the crowd was very different then. I'm not at all convinced that this is a suitable venue for any hymn; but surely this one is the least appropriate. "Fast falls the even tide" it begins. In the middle of the afternoon. The hymn is in fact a gloomy reflection upon the transience of life's sorrows; written by a person, Henry Lyte, often described as neurotic, a week or two before his death from tuberculosis.

If it was enjoyed as community singing in those distant relatively entertainment-free days, there seems little justification for it now, I note, rendered on a TV trailer, by "The Songs of Praise Choir"! Abide with me, is a rather sad hymn, but one of my favourites which I always enjoyed singing in the choir in chapel at Evensong even though I was—am—an unbeliever. But that's just the point. There's a time and place …

Some years ago *The Daily Telegraph* rejected (as they so often do) one of my letters, on this subject. Perhaps they may been put off by my description of "the bellowing godless multitude". But I remain unrepentant.

64

There was a letter in the paper last week from somebody in West Wickham. That name took me back a few years to what must have been 1927 or

1928 when I went to West Wickham to qualify for my Boy Scout cooking badge. These badges were sewn on our upper sleeves and the aim was to collect as many as possible. Anyway, one afternoon, or possibly early evening, we—the Bulldog Scout troop with our blue and yellow insignia set out for what I seem to recall as a quite rural spot, now just a part of the Borough of Bromley. I think we were on the train and the name Elmers End sticks in my memory as one of the stations en route. I think one of the buses used to have a destination sign "Elmers End Garage". Was it the 75? We presumably were herded by one of the Masters at my Prep school who, I imagine, was also a Scoutmaster. It may have been one of the Irish Gray brothers—like Jacob and Esau, one a hairy man and one a smooth man. I had elected to cook sausages as my dish. Not exactly cordon bleu (or what I prefer to call Gordon Blue) but adventurous enough for a small boy of nine or ten.

In any case, one of the major hazards of the cooking badge was that you had to produce your own fire—using no paper and *only one* match. This was, I suppose, one of the practical aspects of scouting like tying different types of knots. (I was never very clever with knots, baffled by Bowline, Clove Hitch etc. though I did master the Reef knot which has remained very useful to me all my life.) But back to the fire. What you had to do was to construct a small tent shape starting with the smallest twigs you could find but increasing in size. It was important to keep one side of the tent open to the wind the direction of which you located by wetting a finger in your mouth and holding it up to feel the cooling breeze. You chopped a few branches to feed the embryonic fire as its flames grew stronger. I think I recall West Wickham as rural because of our ability to find wood of various sizes.

I apparently succeeded with my one match—and by the way, it was just an ordinary match, not one of the enormous ones you can buy these days. Over my now respectable flames I warmed the frying pan I'd brought from home, and into it I placed a number of Sainsbury's pork sausages (pricked to avoid bursting). Carefully turned until cheerfully brown all around, they were then praised and consumed by all. I had gained my badge! I have one of my mother's uninspired snaps of me in my scout uniform. A weedy little creature dwarfed by my large scout hat. I remember the picture's location, our back garden at Andros in front of the May tree and the blackberries. Something about me puts me in mind of those newsreels showing the Herrenfolk herding small Jewish boys from the ghetto on to the waiting trains. Just luck, I remind myself, that I wasn't one of them.

One of the sadnesses of my old age is my apparent inability to enjoy pork sausages. I buy the best grades and cook them to perfection but alas, that potent, porky, flavour has gone; as has the flavour of most food. I remember Bill and I agreeing that we only ate because one had to take on fuel and how little pleasure one gained from even the tastiest dishes.

For my birthday, Zena always gave me roast duck and "words" (of one Syllabub) for pudding and I do still enjoy roast duck; and Dover sole—but nowadays preferably as cooked by my wartime girlfriend, fried in butter with lemon butter sauce. (And, of course, her Dover sole were caught off the coast a mile or two from her home, and sold the same day.) She has moved from the coast now, so I'm afraid those soles are going to have to go into the memory bank.

65

Last Saturday I was to spend a long weekend in Cornwall. Pete had found us a penthouse in St Ives and coffee was to be taken on Sunday (the longest day of the year) with the Robinsons in Porthcothan. Because my back had been very painful, I had appointments on Tuesday with Dominic, the skilful chiropractor who's looked after me for about twenty years and Janet my wonderful masseuse. I did notice that—unusually—I was in a good deal of pain after the treatments, but sometimes you have to wait a day or two for improvement. So, on Saturday at six a.m. I got out of bed and as I stood up was riven by the most fearsome knifelike pain in my back. I let out an involuntary yell and continued to do so with each step I took and putting on my clothes. The phone rang. It was my neighbour Val who wanted to know if I was alright having heard my cries! I was reminded of the poem by James Stephens: "I hear a sudden cry of pain. There is a rabbit in a snare".

By eight, I could move, gingerly, about the world. Pete and Andrew arrived, packed up my car which we were going to use and strapped me into the front seat. (Richard, meanwhile had decided to go by train because he had to return earlier than us.)

We decided to stop first at Amesbury where Pete and I had discovered a rather pleasant little café on one of our trips to Larkhill.

It soon became clear that I was struggling and when Richard phoned on my mobile, he and Pete (and Andrew) decided that we'd have to abort the mission and return home. I have to admit that though I was very disappointed I did feel a certain relief to be returning to my home and my bed (and my cat). I felt very bad about wrecking the holiday for the others, but it really was a case of bowing to the inevitable. I managed to get an appointment with my doctor on the Tuesday, only to discover, alas, that she is leaving at the end of the month. I am sad. Ever since our first meeting (about 10 years ago) she has been so kind and considerate. She wrote me a wonderful letter after reading *SITU*. I'm lucky that I now have another doctor who has looked after me when Dr J. was away. This is another lady doctor, also sympatico. They have arranged an MRI scan and I've just been phoned to say it will be on *Sunday*, 5 July. And people (well, some people) say the NHS is "broken".

66

As I crossed the Broadway yesterday I was accosted by two women; one, quite young and pretty, the other her mother perhaps. They were called Julia and Cecile the young one told me, and from a local church—I didn't catch which. "We've seen you in pain", she said "and we'd like to pray for you". I told her I was an unbeliever and old enough to have seen much of life—and death. It didn't matter, I gathered, and so I said what's to lose. "May I touch you", she asked, taking my arm and with that, closed her eyes and prayed very earnestly for three of four minutes. "Open your arms, Jesus, and ease the pain in Jack's back; and Jack, open *your* arms to Jesus and he will come with you". In due course she finished. "Thank you" I said. "You're good people", and limped off to the car park. And the back pain? I'm afraid Jesus was otherwise engaged.

67

Rummaging the other day in a folder containing some of my early writing, I came across "The Seven Ages of Man—A CAMEO". I believe I was seventeen or eighteen when I wrote this, a series of little stories based on the speech from *As You Like It*. I was curious to see what I had written about old age, having reached it myself. This, then, is how I interpreted the sixth age when I was somewhere around the third.

PANTALOON

The old man sat on the park bench in the pale October sunshine. Before him on the grass, a few small boys and girls scampered like butterflies, calling shrilly to one another.

The sere leaves the wind drove among them fell like a restless carpet on the grass.

The old man peered rheumily at them, called to them, but they did not hear; the gusty wind swept his voice to the treetops, whipping the decaying leaves from branches stark against the winter-boding sky.

Sighing, he got up and shuffled away, leaning on a knobbly stick, a shabby coat about his shoulders.

And he heard the sweet, cruel voices of childhood, shed by the wind in broken cries about him, like gulls round a departing ship.

My father I think with my agreement, sent this off to someone he knew called Sydney Gutman who was involved—possibly a founder of The Bermondsey Bookshop—in 1925, and a celebrated local landmark. In due course this little work came back edited by SG in a way which I, possibly in unjustifiable youth, found rather annoying!

To give you a few examples from "Pantaloon" where I'd written "a restless carpet" he suggested "improvised" which completely lost the implied movement. And instead of "winter-boding sky" which is, perhaps a bit florid, he suggested "leaden" which is, I think, well … leaden. And misses the intended implication of the forthcoming winter of the old man.

And in the last paragraph he put a pencil right through "shed by the wind in broken cries" which, even today I don't feel deserves it. But maybe I'm wrong. SG was a bit literal. For example in *The Infant* I described its disturbance in the cinema as a "squawk". He crossed it out and substituted "cry".

In The Schoolboy, I had described the coming daylight "where twenty three other boys lay sleeping, dead for a season, as the iron December day paled on the ceiling". SG crossed all that out.

In *The Lover*, the wretched boy "grabbed her hand, his heart stamping". SG preferred "thumping". I still prefer my version!

Altogether *The Seven Ages* underwent a fairly severe treatment and in fairness I suppose it was a bit jejune but—possibly—hinted at some future talent!

I think Sydney Gutman must have had a hand in some publishing because I remember that my sister Bé, who was quite a talented artist had an illustration accepted for a short story by, I think, H. G. Wells, called *The Truth about Pyecraft*. Bé drew fat Mr Pyecraft, who had lost gravity, spread-eagled on the ceiling. She had a habit while drawing, of sticking her tongue in the side of her cheek and chewing thin air.

Something else I recall about Bé was how she used to eat a whole bag of violet creams (particularly sickly chocolates) in one afternoon as she lay on her bed, reading a book in her room.

Poor Bé had rather a sad end. She used to express a wish at the start of each new yearly diary that she could meet a swift ending in her sleep. No such luck. She had a rather severe stroke which made speaking difficult when Richard and I went to see her in the local cottage hospital. Only an inspired friend gave her some final happiness with a child's woolly tabby cat. Bé nursed it fondly—remembering, perhaps, her two plump tabbies, Victoria and Albert who lived with her in Wimbledon years before.

68

Had my MRI scan. Not quite what I expected, having only seen it on one of my hospital soaps where the machine seemed quite large, not as claustrophobic as in real life. Also, it turned out to be quite noisy. There's a form to be completed (mainly about previous surgery etc.) and they make sure that you have no metal in you.

Some concern expressed about a shell splinter remaining in my leg after I was wounded in 1945. You were invited to lie on a narrow bed which was then inserted into a tunnel—rather like a torpedo into its tube; and just about as close-fitting. You were given ear plugs and large headphones. Once inside I opened my eyes to see a white curved ceiling with several slots—one of which blew cold air into my left eye. Then the noise started: TooorCAH, tooorCAH, whooma, whooma, grindy grindy. This went on for what seemed a long time, each separate sound having two cycles. The whole procedure took about twenty minutes though—unsurprisingly—it seemed like longer with this deafening orchestra surrounding you. Probably this is why you're given an extended lead with a rubber ball on the end, and urged to press it in case of any worries. This is an intercom with the operators and I can believe it must be a comfort if you suffer from claustrophobia.

It was pleasant to emerge into a warm, sunny Sunday, hoping that this amazing machine will find out why my back is hurting. And that, maybe, something can be done about it.

69

The weather last Sunday was wet and rather cold; "unseasonable" according to the forecasters. I drove home from Richard's, had some lunch, and—because the unseasonable weather discouraged any thought of a walk—lay down on my bed to read the new *Speccie*. It was not long before I was joined by Mina, pointing supple and shining southwards from my lap to where her chin lay draped across my knee. Ten past two and I start to read. After a few minutes I glance at my clock radio: ten to *four*. Yes, anaesthetised by my warm little cat, I have dozed off.

As I grow older, this tends to happen more often than I want and I fight against it. I remember that Bill used to tell me recently that he fell asleep often in the daytime. And, indeed, I recall more than one occasion on which he dozed off as we were talking.

Scott, too, when I visited him in the local care home, often refused to open his eyes, and sat nodding in silence.

"When you are old and grey and full of sleep" wrote W. B. Yeats, and it's true that—devoid of much motivation—you are. So I try to find something to keep this sleep at bay and usually go for a rather pointless walk, rather than wind down even more quickly towards that sleep from which there is no awakening.

Thinking, as I often do, about dying, I wasn't so sure that Dylan Thomas was on the right track when he urged us to "rage against the dying of the light". I can see an argument for a young person to do so, but there comes a time (or anyway, I think it will) when you realise that it's time to depart; and, if you're lucky, to do so peacefully and accepting. And, if all this sounds a bit gloomy I can only say that when you approach your hundredth year, you'll probably share these feelings yourself.

Still, today the sun is shining, it is warm and I shall go for a walk and put aside thoughts of my (presumably not-too-distant) demise.

70

Oh dear, the football season is nearly on us again. TV commercials are full of spectators displaying almost orgasmic pleasure as a goal is scored, and there is M. Henry explaining why the football league is the best in the world. I am still a (rather lukewarm) supporter of Arsenal, a sort of hardwired harking back, I suppose, to my days on the Highbury Terrace. But I do really find the football scene rather disgusting. When you see young working class boys being paid £140,000 a *week* and you think of people on whom we depend—the bus drivers, the dustmen, the postmen, the surgeons, almost anyone I suppose when you come down to it—handing out that sort of money for kicking a football—however skilfully, is absurd. I hasten to say (in case you might think otherwise) that I do not envy these young men at all. By and large I regard a footballer's life as dangerous and rather pointless: just like owning half a dozen expensive cars.

I remember the first £1,000 footballer and I do find it disgusting to see them being transferred now for fifty million or more, soon to reach a hundred I'm sure, in a world where children die for lack of a cup of clean water, a handful of pounds can avert blindness and much of the world goes hungry every day. Yes, I suppose I've become naive in my old age. But there's still right and wrong—even if most of the world seems to be on the wrong bit.

71

Along with many others I have been reading about Mr Palmer, the despicable dentist who recently killed Cecil, a sort of landmark lion lured out of its protected park area in Zimbabwe. The wretched man was, apparently, only concerned that what he had done was "legal" (and had cost him some huge sum of US dollars).

You'll know from what I've written earlier, my feelings of disgust and hostility towards any cruelty to animals. What I simply can't comprehend is the mindset of someone who wants to kill the large cats, the most beautiful, most graceful of all the animals. There were other pictures of this man with another large lion he'd killed and a leopard, its once lithe, spotted body draped over his arm, paws limp in death.

I mean, once you've set aside any commercial or "prestigious" consideration, what gives you the desire to *kill*—as opposed to admire— these wonderful creatures? I can see that culling certain groups of deer, for example, does ensure the health of the survivors (and provide food) but I find even this unpleasant when you see the sort of nobility of a stag. There was a great poem by John Davidson, Victorian poet and playwright, which I read as quite a young boy about "a stag, a runnable stag" which, after being chased for 30 miles drowned rather than be caught.

> Three hundred gentlemen, able to ride,
>> Three hundred horses as gallant and free,
> Beheld him escape on the evening tide,
>> Far out till he sank in the Severn Sea,
>> Till he sank in the depths of the sea—
>>> The stag, the buoyant stag, the stag
>>> That slept at last in a jewell'd bed
>>> Under the sheltering ocean spread,
>>> The stag, the runnable stag.

Then there is fox hunting. I could never do this even though I used to be a good enough rider. I was deterred once and for all at Christmas 1934, when one of my presents was the complete poems of John Masefield. One of these was *Reynard the Fox*, heart-racingly exciting, where (thank god) a fox finally goes to earth after a chase which even the pursuers describe as never to be forgotten.

I do accept that foxes are destructive, especially if you keep chickens, and have to be kept under control. And I do accept that death by a pack of hounds is, though quick, rather barbaric; but preferable to a gunshot wound and a slow, solitary painful death.

Although I have killed in war and at long range, I did experience an occasion when I might have done so close up and person to person. To establish an O.P., I have climbed to a church tower in Holland, arriving tired and out of breath when a German soldier burst out of cover just below and ran zigzagging, for his life. I seized my rifle and got three shots at him, but being exhausted by my climb, couldn't steady myself and missed Fritz who disappeared into the nearby wood. He was a bit lucky because I was captain of the school shooting eight and no mean performer. If I had been carrying my liberated German Schmeisser machine pistol, he wouldn't have been so lucky. Later in life, I was rather glad I hadn't killed this wretched fellow, an ordinary solder like myself, not like one of those guards who sang "We are the boys of Treblinka" in the film *Shoah*. I would still shoot them today though, of course, it's too late.

72

A unanimous cascade of praise marked the obituary of Cilla Black who died recently. Conspicuously dissenting was catty old Noel Coward who found her "ghastly beyond words".

My own reaction to the talented creature came when I loved her version of *Anyone who had a heart*—so much better than the original American artist. Later—and more or less accidentally—I saw bits of *Blind Date*, which I thought was one of the most sniggeringly unpleasant bits of TV I've had the misfortune to view.

73

A newly discovered pleasure: watching Prom concerts on TV. I have been surprised by how much the music has been enhanced by sights of the movement of the many instruments—some which I can't even identify by name. Of course, they are all gleaming; and there's something particularly uplifting to see a group of long silver trumpets shining out their triumphant notes. Another wind instrument I particularly enjoy is circular with four or five tubes within it. No idea what this is called but it makes a fruitful sound. I also enjoy the synchronised sweep of the violins (and violas I presume, not knowing the difference). I suppose you could call theirs the sweetest music. The sight of the long bows which caress the cellos is a bit like the stroking of my cat Mina; slow, soothing. What a contrast in the percussion section, particularly the sticks which look like tennis bats, plied with dazzling speed and beating out ponderous, threatening sound unlike the rapid tattoo of ordinary drumsticks.

Sometimes you see a pair of delicate hands plucking the strings of an enormous harp behind which you glimpse a shadowy face. And the hands at the piano; rushing from one end of the keys to the other, unexpectedly curved almost like claws as the fingers fly up and down. I find this kind of dexterity almost unbelievable. The conductor's demeanour also adds to the mood of the music. Sometimes there is also one very large wind instrument with a huge gaping mouth. I don't think that it participates frequently as it sits alongside the trombones which I always enjoy with their piston-like sliding to and fro and their (to me) surprisingly emollient sound.

He (or she) seems sometimes almost in a trance, at others alight with enthusiasm, almost threatening, always drawing out particular moods from the various sections of the orchestra.

When I watch the Proms I'm reminded of two of my life's ambitions, neither of which I achieved: to fly an aeroplane and to be a concert pianist. It's probably just as well that I never learned to fly as I have a feeling that I wouldn't have survived the war. As to the piano; as a small boy, I had lessons but I don't think I showed much aptitude—or perhaps lacked the will to concentrate or the desire to succeed. All I can remember at this very long range is that one lot of keys (was it?) was E G B D F (every good boy deserves favours) and the other A C E G (all cats eat grapes).

Anyway, lazy or inept, I did not progress unlike my mother and Elly— who could go to the cinema and sit down at the piano and play the music from the films. How I envied her. How I still do!

74

The Germans it seems, are going to take in about 800,000 Mediterranean refugees, while we are vilified for our apparent hostility to the few thousand would-be invaders at Calais. I'm not quite sure how many times larger Germany is than us, but there must be plenty of space available. Also, although refuge—potentially life itself—is offered to nearly a million people, life was taken, scientifically and systematically, from at least five times that number of innocent people in the not very distant past. So in my book, Germany is still at least four million souls in debt. Nor, by comparison, should our record over the centuries be criticised harshly.

75

So, the words I hoped never to write: Peg has died. I had always (rather selfishly) hoped that *she* would be the one to receive the same news about *me*.

Apparently she came well through successful keyhole heart surgery—performed by amazingly lucky coincidence by a world-wide expert working in a nearby hospital. Later, things went wrong and she gradually shut down. Her end was peaceful. I'm so glad.

76

A couple of random thoughts about my life (lives?) with Peg. As an urban creature, my first experience of seeing asparagus grow was in her garden. Also one autumn, could it have been just after the war? I helped her pick apples from her little orchard and wrap each individually in newspaper for storage through the coming winter. Some were Bramley, I remember, and the others succulent Cox's orange.

Jane, Peg's daughter relates in *A Figure in the Sand*, her moving account of her search for her father's desert grave, how she visited Zena and me in 1988. She still had a tattered copy of Beatrix Potter's story of *Johnny Townmouse* which I had given her some forty years earlier. She quoted Peg as follows: "It was a joke between us. Jack was so like the town mouse, so neat and well dressed, and I was like the country mouse, all plump and dishevelled".

I retained this persona and often signed birthday cards etc. "Townmouse, J" army fashion. On the shelf above my bed is a pristine copy of *Johnny Townmouse*, sent to me by Peg in recent years.

I feel a twinge of disloyalty dwelling on my past with her, but, as I've told my boys, I never regretted for one instant my marriage to my "unique Canadian" to whom, in my last book, I devoted many times the coverage of this little chapter.

77

Another obituary in the *Telegraph* last week caught my eye: "EVELYN MONIER- WILIAMS, SYMPATHETIC JUDGE WHO TOOK A LENIENT STANCE WHEN SENTENCING". It then filled two columns covering his life, including his service as a field gunner; which is where our lives converged in November 1942.

Yet it was almost exactly sixty three years later that I received a long letter from him, outlining our shared experience—he with 50 Div and I with 51st—across Africa, Sicily, Normandy, the Ardennes, the Rhine Crossing "thrown in for good measure" as he put it. He mentions Lawrie Wilde (a fellow barrister) who, with Patricia and family were neighbours and good friends of ours, all now departed, in Lansdowne Road.

He ends, concentrating on an episode touched on in my earlier books.

One of my happiest recollections was on the *Niew Amsterdam* when we vyed in friendly rivalry for the favours of the beautiful wife of an absent English Diplomat—but that, as they say, is another story!

All the best and my gratitude to you for writing a truly magnificent book.

Yours ever.

Bill

I realise, from his obituary, that he was a widower by the time he wrote. I had a long phone call to him but we never got together again; something I now regret … with so much over the years.

78

After a few weeks darkened by incessant back ache, the happy prospect of a weekend in Cornwall. The weather prospect could be described as "iffy" so how uplifting to be greeted by warm sunshine and blue skies. On our first evening, we made for the very fine beach near the rather luxurious house Pete had found for us on the Internet. It was the sort of day that Masefield must have had in mind when, in *Sea Fever*, he wrote that all he asked was "a fair wind, and the white clouds flying / And the flung spray and the blown spume / and the seagulls crying". It was nearly high tide and the huge white rollers sent us scurrying for dry land as the sea rushed up the beach. (Scurrying is hardly a description of my stick-aided scramble to safety.)

The sight of this foaming sea reminded me—rather incongruously—of my first visit to Cornwall in what must have been the early thirties. I'm not sure how it came about that my mother and I took a coach to the West Country, ending up one early evening at a hotel in Newquay. (Our coach was nothing like the rather splendid vehicles Zena and I trundled in quite late in our lives. These earlier ones were called charabancs and were vaguely lower class. We called them Sharras.) Anyway, bidding Ma farewell, I donned swimming trunks and made my way down to the beach in what I seem to recall was the hotel's private lift. At the bottom was assorted sea gear including surf boards. I seized one of these and emerged onto the beach (private?) where I was confronted by threatening white

rollers. I had never used a surf board, but—so young then, so fearless!—
dashed into the angry sea, launched myself on to a likely looking wave
and sank like a stone. Eventually, I timed it right, and then came that
magical, almost flying sensation shoreward. It was there that I became
forever enslaved by the swooping board and the feel of the wave lifting
me, lifting me. I taught the boys to surf, at first clinging to my back like
little monkeys, later surpassed by their skill and stamina. The other surfing
memory triggered by the rollers that evening took me back to one evening
probably in the fifties when Mervyn and I looked out on the splendid
surf at Porthcothan and—careless of the furious wind and approaching
darkness—made for the beach and one of the most exciting times I can
remember. Later we lay in hot baths and consumed gin and tonic to
restore life and limb. Ah, that howling sea, almost boiling against you as
you fought the swooping, bouncing board.

On Porthtowan Beach, Cornwall, September 2015. *Left to right*: Pete, Jack, and Richard.

Little did I think back then (and just as well perhaps) of the limping old thing I would become all those years later.

Still, enough of the self-pity. I am at least able to manage a rather slow walk every day, to drive, albeit not as far as once, and to find some pleasure still in life; remembering that three out of four of my ninety year old friends have died recently. It's still a moment which occasions a certain surprise seeing the daylight in the morning.

79

"Seeing the daylight in the morning" was something I welcomed a couple of nights ago. I had been awake all night with a nasty little hacking cough, which, as morning broke, left me unable to make a sound. For some reason it sent me back to an evening in 1934 or perhaps 1935 which became legendary in our family as THE NIGHT WITTING COUGHED. Our Mr Witting (I think his first name was Arthur) was a regular member of the people who made up Bridge fours of an evening in the drawing room at Andros. I can also remember Gerald C., who, my father told me (a year or two later) had wanted to make me a Mason. His wife, Claire, was a sweet, timid little woman, not a very confident Bridge player—and clearly terrified when partnering my father—an efficient but a dreadfully intolerant partner.

But about Witting, whose son, Clifford, became a quite well known— and probably underrated author of no less than sixteen detective stories. Witting was a heavy smoker; one of those with a cigarette more or less permanently drooping from his lower lip.

Bridge was played in a haze of tobacco smoke. Apart from the non-stop Witting cigarettes, my Pa puffed on one of his Dunhill pipes or, occasionally a Romeo and Julietta cigar. None of the ladies smoked but sat wreathed in what was later vilified as passive smoke.

Unsurprisingly, Witting tended to cough quite frequently, but on the memorable occasion on which he entered our annals, he had the most fearful and uncontrollable fit. Gasping, red faced, he whooped and bellowed for what seems in my boyhood memory to have been for about ten minutes, though it was almost certainly less.

Eventually—assisted by gulps of the rather decent whisky which was always on offer—he managed to stop.

Some years later, I discovered that Mr Witting had—not unsurprisingly—died of lung cancer. There can't have been a more likely candidate. (Made me glad that I puffed on my last fag on 8 October 1983.)

80

I see that Denis Healey has died aged 98. I never met him, but went out occasionally with his wife Edna when we were at Oxford. I think that—with some justification—she didn't look on me as a serious long-term prospect.

The nineties seem to be a hazardous decade. My four friends have all died on that "Century" straight, the tape in sight, but finally, faltering and falling. Somehow, it seems reminiscent of the 1908 London Olympic Marathon, when the leader, a tiny 22 year old pastry chef, Dorando Pietri fell about half a dozen times with a mere 400 yards to go. Assisted, he staggered over the line but was disqualified; though Queen Alexandra, a much-moved spectator, later presented him with a silver cup.

Nobody to help *us* over the line though. Something which is on my mind a bit frequently these days.

81

A fuckstream pours from my mouth echoing (complementing?) the blood streaming from the middle finger I have carelessly cut. This, in itself, was not so remarkable. I've often cut a finger in recent years, but not in this particularly clumsy way. Putting on my trousers, I felt a lurch to my left and, fearing a fall, clutched the arm of my wicker bedroom chair; a good move but badly executed. The inside of my middle finger scraped the wood and the blood flowed.

The incident seemed to me to typify the minor hazards which, increasingly, beset my declining years. For example, the numerous pills which I take have the habit of ejecting like fighter pilots from the bubbles from which I push them; and travel inexplicably large distances to find shelter under my bed, on the heating pipes or anywhere which makes it difficult for me to retrieve them. Often it's the next day before I find one lurking slyly in some fold of material.

Quite often I pick something up and for no very good reason, drop it. Or a certain shirt button simply refuses to go into its designated buttonhole. Or it takes me half a dozen times to produce an acceptable knot for my tie: possibly because I so rarely wear one these days. (In fact, I have totally forgotten how to tie a bow tie; something which matters less these days when my use of a dinner jacket is but a distant memory.)

I share the frustration voiced from time to time in the letter column of my daily paper, over the difficulty of opening almost anything nowadays. My favourite mints are so tightly encased in film that even when I've found a place where I can open it, the film is so tight that I need scissors or a very sharp knife to gain entry.

As for screwtops … I should be lost without the splendid Brabantia opener which Carey gave me ages ago for Christmas.

Reluctantly, I accept the limitations of old age. No more standing on chairs or ladders I promise my sons (after falling off one recently). I rely on my kind neighbours to change light bulbs or shift garden shelfing. Sometimes—if my back is particularly troublesome—I even ask someone to make my bed.

Still, I have to remind myself, at least you aren't dead. Not by any means really.

82

I've been experiencing what I could (inaccurately) call my Rosebud syndrome. On my mind has been the elusive name which was the last word of *Citizen Kane*, the eponymous hero of Orson Welles's great film.

I wasn't thinking so much of my own last word as some rather obscure incidents of my past life. I don't mean those predicable high points which would be known to my family and a few friends, but moments now known only to me. Perhaps the earliest: I must have been four or five and in a cot or small bed in my parents' bedroom (always known as the billiard room) at Andros. I had diphtheria and in my delirium thought that a huge stone came rolling round the picture rail to fall on me. I used to scream in terror. I remember that my hands also seem to grow large and heavy and threaten to crush me. The doctor came in the night and drew fluid from my back. I think he was called Dr Gilchrist. After he retired, our next doctor was Wheeler O'Brien, father of Wilfred, a boyfriend of my sister Elly. However, he married a rather glamorous film actress called Elizabeth Allen. (Dr Gilchrist, a dour Scottish protestant, lived rather inappropriately in a pleasant corner house, No. 1 Jews Walk, off Kirkdale Road, on the way to Forest Hill.) One day when I was, I suppose about eleven or twelve, I was walking home along Jews Walk with the electric motor boat I'd been sailing on the pond at Horniman's Museum. I was accosted by three or four threatening young louts who demanded to have a look at my boat. Needless to say, they made off with it.

I did run round to the police station in Dartmouth Road to report the incident. The police, as I recall, were quite pleasant but it was clear that they had no intention of doing anything about it. I repeated all this to Pa when I got home and I think he did contact the police but with no more result than me.

I'm sure this event has led to the fury I have always felt against bullies like that. And, according to the daily press reports, the attitude of the cops doesn't seem to have changed that much either!

Next: I must have been about six or seven. I am standing on the first floor landing at Andros on my way to the hall, down a quite large flight of stairs. I step off the first one and suddenly I am at the bottom with no recollection of walking down. It was as if I stepped off the first flight and flew down to the hall with no memory of the journey itself. I have no explanation of how or why this happened. I can only describe the event— still clearly recalled—all these years later.

83

Something occurs to me which underlines how things change. On that landing at Andros was the bathroom, serving at one time my parents, my sisters, my brother and myself. Its source of hot water was an ancient geyser which had to be lighted and produced a ponderous stream of hot water. I can't remember how often but I do remember that it was temperamental and sometimes difficult to keep alight. Not impressive as a source of ablution for a house with seven bedrooms (including the nursery) two of which were in the attic region for Lizzie the cook and Jessie the original nurse ("Nag", the nurse and general housemaid described in my earlier memoir). They—I suppose—were expected to undertake their ablutions on one of their one and a half days off each week. Nor did we have running water in our bedrooms. There was a washstand with a basin which fitted into a circular hole, for which warm water was provided (presumably by poor Nag) every morning.

Later—in the mid-thirties—my father made a rather spectacular profit—perhaps £40,000 in today's money—through some shares called Dorman Long; and invested some by installing a large new bathroom in what had been the nursery in my infancy. By then, my sisters had married and departed, so the huge new bath and basin were freely available. I still recall the blissful, full length soaking in ample hot water, when returning home late at night after an evening in town. My own bath nowadays is too small for such indulgence so I tend to use a shower instead.

84

But to return to the third remembered moment. I was opening the batting for the school eleven against the old boys; always a testing fixture since they had all been first eleven players—and knew our weaknesses. On this occasion I was facing a fast bowler who had bullied me and made my life misery when I first joined the school. Down came a fast in-swinger just outside the off stump. I leaned into it and effortlessly stroked it to the boundary. It was one of those rare moments of batting perfection. The bowler looked stunned. Unfortunately, I have to admit that a few overs later he got me out LBW. As I walked back to the pavilion I met the headmaster. "I thought that off drive would be too much for you Jack", he said. Maybe; but eighty years on I still feel the bat connect as the ball skims to boundary ropes.

First XI cricket team at Weymouth College, 1936. The author is second from left in the back row.

85

There's been a good deal of discussion in the papers recently about "elderly" car drivers. Should they be retested at 70? 75? Should they undergo a similar medical? Should they even be on the road? As this has a very pertinent application to my life, I've been following the subject with interest. I see that "elderly" relates to drivers aged 75 to 80, or maybe just five more. What about me then—98 early in 2016? Not to mention the 191 centenarians which the omniscient Google tells me still drive in the UK. Well, I'll be frank. I'm not as good a driver as I was say fifty years ago, but I do regard myself as a safe driver as I sit in my 1.6 Clio, rarely exceeding 60 mph on the big roads, but with plenty of Va Va Voom if I need it. I still back into a small parking space as competently as I did when I was young. But I do have to concentrate more than of old when judging space to pass or meeting oncoming traffic. (The latter is particularly true in Wimbledon where I live, as the roads are infested with large 4 × 4's, usually driven by childbearing women carrying small children to our numerous schools. These "yummy mummies" as they are called, do have the habit of driving with their wheels over the middle white line. Living here, you learn to live with that and keep out of the way.)

I've owned fourteen (I think) cars in my life, the most glamorous of which was, probably, a 2.5 litre Daimler Jaguar which I drove too fast from time to time.

I started to drive when I was about twelve and one of my early experiences was with my brother-in-law Lawrie's Swift—a cumbersome old thing with a "dicky" at the back, seating an extra passenger. Getting to a low gear or steep hills you had to "double-de-clutch"—quite tricky on, say, Reigate Hill, where there was never any certainty of reaching the top. I have the impression that this became unnecessary after something called synchromesh arrived. Of course, cars are incomparably better equipped and more comfortable than before the Second World War, but at what price! A friend of mine bought a second-hand car in 1937 for £5; and drove it to Edinburgh.

I've had four (minor) accidents—all since 1945. One was my fault, the other three were not, and I had my costs met by the other parties; though in one case I had to take a major insurance company to court, when I (brilliantly!) won my case.

I've been found guilty once of speeding (48 mph) by the Wimbledon Tennis Courts early one morning sometime in the 1950s. I had a new Austin Westminster and didn't realise how much larger and faster it was than its predecessor. My licence was endorsed for three years. No points in those days. My other clashes with the law have involved parking in its numerous methods of unpleasantness.

I've decided to spare you details of some of my clashes with wardens with whom I am at unending war; though now greatly relieved by my Blue Badge disabled concession.

On balance, as I've said, I now regard myself as a safe driver. I sit placidly giving in to others, even if I have the right of way. If some idiot passes me while over the limit, I let him (it's usually a him). I should think that the number of times I use the hooter in one year could be counted on the fingers of two hands—or possibly even one.

My current driving licence takes me to 2018, but whether I'll still be at the wheel—or life's wheel—who knows?

86

Next week it'll be two years since Richard gave me Mina, my tabby cat, as a Christmas present—high on the shortlist of Best Ever. Except when the weather was warm and sunny, Mina has spent most of the day (and all night) with me.

Her routine suits us both. She awaits me at the bathroom door in the morning and, on my cry of "Doods" shoots downstairs with speed and agility which contrasts sadly with my own rather slow and—is there such a word?—unconfident progress. (A fall when I missed the bottom stair a year or two ago has made me particularly cautious.)

After sampling her meal Mina sits on the kitchen counter watching me make tea and toast. As soon as I butter and marmalade it she jumps down and eats more. Boring detail? Of course, but it becomes the stuff of close companionship—a boon in one's last time. I've had to woo Mina. She—a rescue cat—came to me nervous and cautious and I kept her in for her first three weeks. After that, she loved freedom to explore the garden (and next door) but—unlike ill-fated Rainbow—doesn't go too far from home. A few poor mice and the odd bird have paid the price of her freedom. She is a very swift predator—even catches flies in the house.

As I say, I've had to woo her. From the first, she enjoyed the gentle head scratching at which I've become so feline-expert. But stroking behind her neck could land you with a sharp little bite. And chest and belly were strictly out of bounds. After two years, I'm allowed full body stroking and an occasional chest rub. But I understand my limits.

Mina has a very quiet purr. In fact, she is the unpurring-est cat I've had. As I only have (had) one good ear, I could hardly hear her though I can feel her vibrating as she lies full length on me from lap to chin dangling over my knee when I lie on my bed in the day to read or watch telly.

Yes, the nerve of one good(ish) ear is now beginning to malfunction, and a hearing aid looms. Still, perhaps it'll help me to hear her. (I rather doubt it.)

This is a cat with a mind of her own and a strong will. Nowhere is this better demonstrated than at bedtime. I usually watch telly till about 10, with Mina sprawled comfortably from my lap southwards. "I'm going to bed now" I tell her, with a gentle nudge. She makes to jump down. "Don't leave, you don't have to leave" I wheedle. But to no avail. As I go to the bathroom for the last pee of the day (or—I hope—the night) she runs off downstairs, possibly for a snack, possibly to show who's in charge.

I go to bed and put out the light. For a while I listen to Radio 4 though this becomes increasingly difficult; muffled by my hearing problem. Also I know that Mina prefers me to put the radio off. This done, I cry out "Mina" a few times, after which I know that I have to wait for her to decide to join me. Sometimes this only takes a minute or two, sometimes ten or more, and occasionally I've fallen asleep alone. But usually, as I'm drifting off I feel her stealthy progress across my pillow, then down the far side of the bed where—having assumed the (foetal) position the bend of my leg awaits and I feel her comforting presence fitting into it.

Off to sleep then for us both; myself at first till between midnight and one, Mina usually till about five, though she returns after ten or fifteen minutes and stays close until I get up at seven-ish.

Reader, if you too live with a cat (note that I don't say "own" a cat. You may own a dog but as they say, a cat has staff) you'll identify with the companionship (and slavery!) that it can offer.

I think that this may be particularly true of rescue animals who learn to trust—perhaps even to love—their saviours. Mina is only a young cat, five years, and perhaps too young for an oldie in his final time. So she likes

Mina. (*Photograph by Andrew McDonald*)

me to pretend to hunt her. I cry out woowoo and flap my arms. She rushes away to hide. I follow. More woowoo until we both get a bit tired (or bored).

As I say, I'm perhaps too old for her but Pete and Andrew (cat people) have promised to take her when I've departed which is a big weight off my mind. Meanwhile I hope to enjoy life with my tabby lady, warm in her favourite spot under the hall radiator or on the window sill there, or just sitting on my chest of drawers by my bedroom window watching the world go by as did her person when he lay there with TB sixty-three years ago.

87

I suppose it's not all that long ago that I might have been described as "that old madman living alone with his cat". I do admit that—like my old dad—I am somewhat eccentric; and, possibly, a bit OCD-prone. This was crossing my mind the other evening as I prepared my breakfast tray for the next morning and realised that Teaspoon was absent. I have six or seven teaspoons but this one has a thin shaft which gives it a certain elegance not shared by the others. Teaspoon is one of several items which are the only ones I use. For example, there is Spoon. There are probably twenty or thirty spoons of various sizes in the kitchen drawer, not to mention some rarely-used sterling silver from my boyhood at Andros. But Spoon, a stainless steel dessert spoon fits my hand so well and is so strong when dividing fruit. Thus, Spoon is the only spoon I use for fruit and other pudding. I'm not quite sure about its origins. I have an uneasy feeling that I may have stolen it. Then there are various knives. A small, sharp one with a black handle is Chappie. Its companion with blue handle (given to me by Maria) is called (what else?) Gainsborough. And until recently, when its blade detached, there was the long sharp thin one called The Poet. I think that you'll see why. I also ought not to forget Bad Spoon, a small utensil made, I think, of Dutch silver, and, as such, another relic of my boyhood. I'm not sure where Bad spoon acquired its title; perhaps because it had become dull and rather unattractive in its old age and nowadays is only allowed to be used for French dressing which I hope, can't damage it any further. So different is

Silvery Top, a hallmarked, elegant boyhood relic which has exclusive access to my breakfast marmalade jar. These utensils are (though I have kitchen drawers full of others) basically the only ones I use along with some small knives with a saw edge, which I bought from a shop called Knights in Esher some time in the eighties when I was working as a bookseller and, later, racing tipster after I had to retire because of age limits (since abolished, I believe). Zena and I used these exclusively for breakfast toast and all main dishes for years and I have continued the custom.

As I have accepted some degree of eccentricity, it is only right to include Swaabese, my private language with its elements of French, German, 1984 and additives of my own devising. Some people regard this as peckle (peculiar). There are examples of Swaabese in my last book, but let me give you a taste of it here. For example, when I use my electric shower, I call out the settings as follows: Low is Lau as in frau. Medium became Meejastudies and High is Higgerty. The road sign Slow Down I prefer to revise as Slough Doan—more full of character somehow. And if I tell you when I come in after my daily walk, that there were Dykles and Tertervallisses, I was describing bright periods and sunny intervals.

There is a certain indefensible originality about my language which applies even to my supper—Poopooseeryay. And Breakfast—Braglingyay. But I can see that people could regard it as eccentric. Surely not mad though?

88

I must add a postscript to my piece about Mina. Coming back from my walk, I lay in Zena's chair as I usually do, to ease the ache in my back. After a few minutes, madam jumped onto my chest, and after making a bit of bread (which is really called kneading) lay down with her nose a few inches from mine, vibrating gently with closing eyes. So touched, so flattered was I by this proximity that I had to close my own eyes and we both had half an hour's nap.

As she lay there while I stroked her neck and back, I felt that the two years she'd lived with me had succeeded in forging the sort of bond you hope to achieve with your pet; particularly a lady cat!

89

"Luckily I still have one good ear" I wrote in chapter 27; but the luck ran out recently. A heavy cold had left my hearing much reduced, woolly and echoing when I spoke. As my "bad" ear had been rated (after nine operations) as having "No Useful Hearing" things were not good. Two courses of pseudoephedrine which had worked in the past were ineffective this time and at a routine visit to ENT I was given a hearing test and told that the nerve in my good ear was not functioning. I should need a hearing aid.

I did find being in effect deaf very depressing, in particular trying to conduct a conversation. The TV subtitles and volume were now being increased to quite alarming numbers, as was the car radio. The phone and the microwave were also virtually inaudible—or, in the case of the one by my bedside—emitting a sort of apologetic squeak.

It's a truism isn't it, that while blindness is a tragedy, deafness is somehow comic. I remember how Zena and I used to listen to a radio comedy in which the late Derek Guyler and someone else played two deaf old gentlemen with the resultant hilarious misunderstandings. I also recall laughing out loud at parts of a novel called *Deaf Sentence*. Needless to say, my attitude has undergone a considerable change.

However, some unexpected help was at hand. Peg's daughter, Wanna and her grandson Jasper decided to send me one of her (very expensive) privately purchased hearing aids. It arrived, *very* small with some even smaller batteries, and even though not made for me does fit in any ear, stays put and dramatically improves my hearing. I think that its tendency to whistle and squeal means that I need to get it adjusted by some local expert who can fill me in on other details. Meanwhile my GP has referred me to the hospital for an *NHS* hearing aid which nowadays is digital and not too obtrusive, unlike the stone age, non-functional model I was given years ago for my bad ear; which, in any case, rejects anything put in it.

So, my life is changing once again. Soon after 5 a.m. I push the hearing aid into my ear, and am able to hear the weather, the *Farming* and the *Today* programmes which, aid-less, had become distorted and no longer intelligible. (The female voices, I should put on the record, were particularly blurred and infuriating.) I sent Wanna an email: "You have brought me back into the world. Thank you."

90

Pete has been in the loft and unearthed a few rather tattered relics relating to my earliest and later education.

I quote a few items which perhaps cast their shadows before. From "South Hill College" which was, I think my kindergarten (and actually 119 Mayoh Road when I lived at No. 93).

I was eight when my Conduct was described as "Good, much too talkative" but Composition and Dictation was "very good for his age". The last one from my prep school is missing but at age eleven, most subjects are good or very good except Algebra and Geometry: "Quite good but is too careless. Inclined to be lazy and untidy".

Finally, my last report from Weymouth College in 1936. For Literature: 1st in form of 11. "Deserves his place. He is genuinely interested and is showing real powers of critical judgement".

And A. G. Pite, my great headmaster summed me up as follows:

He has had a varied school career. He has rendered most useful service in many ways and I am sad that his time here is over. If he sticks to the principles in which he really believes he should do very well both at Oxford and after.

I have never been convinced that I have done very well, but at least, like Othello, "I have done the State some service...".

Another item is a menu dated 9 November 1943 when I was returning from Sicily and war in the desert on an American troopship. A diary entry for 10 November in my book *Field of Fire* reads: "Meals are only two daily—for us 0830 and 1800 but they are so enormous that they keep one pretty well stocked up for the intervening hours ... and guaranteed to produce indigestion of the acutest variety". You must remember that we had lived basically on bully beef and hard tack for most of the preceding year and were quite unable to cope with this abundance.

AMERICAN REPUBLICS LINE
S. S. "ARGENTINA"

BREAKFAST

Iced Fruit Juice

Kadota Figs in Syrup   Stewed Fruit
Cream of Wheat   Puffed Wheat
Corn Flakes   Puffed Rice   Shredded Wheat   Bran Flakes
Steamed Salt Herring, Melted Butter
EGGS: Boiled   Fried   Scrambled
American Bacon   Premium Ham
Pan Fried Potatoes
Fruit Muffins   Fresh Rolls   Assorted Buns   Toast
Orange Marmalade   Assorted Fruit Jams
Coffee   Tea

SUPPER

Sweet Relish   Bismarck Herring   French Sardines in Oil
Olives   Canape City
Potage Americaine
Baked Fresh Mackerel, Spanish Sauce
Macaroni au Gratin
Saute of Chicken with Red & Green Peppers
Roast Fresh Jersey Ham, Dish Gravy, Apple Sauce
Braised Onions   Smothered Red Cabbage
Mashed or Baked Potatoes
Assorted Cold Cuts, Chow Chow
Cole Slaw
Apple Tapioca Pudding   Ice Cream   Assorted Cookies
Cheese and Crackers
Fresh Fruit
Coffee   Tea

Tuesday, November 9th, 1943

The menu from SS *Argentina*, signed by the author and travelling companions.

91

As I started this book at the end of 2013, I finish it at the end of 2015. So I thought that as "the year is dying, let it die" to quote (once again) *In Memoriam*, this might be a suitable time to finish it. I have to admit I shall rather miss grumbling about so many things (on paper of course; I've no doubt I shall continue to inflict my telephone and email rants on long-suffering family and friends).

It has been a year in which I have lost oldest and closest friends. Indeed, I now have but one contemporary ninety-four-year-old friend whose prospects are not very promising. I have written earlier about the final struggle of us nonagenarians to the finishing tape. As another year looms I am very aware of the inevitable deterioration of some of my own physical—and mental—functions. One was made very clear to me as today I walked—limped—round my daily walk circuit which now takes me five minutes longer than it did a year or two ago. That said, I realise how lucky I am even to be able to do my daily walk and to drive my car without difficulty. I can see pretty well but wish I could hear better. I'm still able to do my own shopping, select the precise bananas I want and recognise which supermarket I prefer for which product.

Sometimes I think what a shame it is to leave the world without finding out all the amazing things that can happen in a few centuries; always (perhaps inadvisably) assuming that our little blue speck in space survives that long. Then I think of the fearful loneliness of having no old friends, no "do you remember" moments. Even today, I note how my several great, great young relatives perceive me as not quite like others. Nor—as I have to remind myself—am I, quite.

I've given a good deal of thought to "God" in my time. As I watch TV programmes about space and our universe and all the other universes, thoughts about beginnings and endings of everything become too difficult to comprehend. All that I've concluded is that man-made religions are quite unbelievable if, in some cases, harmless, and responsible for much of the world's ills. I like to describe myself as an agnostic atheist if that isn't, or even if it is, an oxymoron. So, I face my remaining limited time in this world trying to enjoy the numerous small pleasures which remain; and after that, when my time to depart has come, let Hamlet speak for me: "The rest is silence".

Jack Swaab, March 2018. (*Photograph by Andrew McDonald*)

Journal Entries, 2017: 'The Home Straight'

15 March 2017

'The Ides of March are come,' says Caesar, a bit snootily, to the soothsayer. 'Aye Caesar, but not gone,' replies the unrepentant fellow. Now, late on this Ides, I am reasonably hopeful of avoiding Caesar's outcome and—pressed by my sons—am going on a little further still with this extra section to mark my 100th birthday. (Tempting fate, I feel.) No numbered chapters this time. Instead, I'll be commenting on something which is in the news or my news—or in the past.

17 March

This is St Patrick's Day and we are due to play the Irish at rugby in Dublin. Don't be surprised if they launch a furious attack from the word go—hoping to frustrate our title hopes as they did a few years ago. We *should* win if only because we have such strong reserves, but don't bet on it; I certainly won't.

18 March

Right for once. (And I backed Chase the Spud, winner of the Midlands Grand National at 11-1, so right twice.)

26 March

Sunday—and last night the clocks went forward an hour. I seem to remember this as when the next day used to feel rather cold. But today as I went on my walk the sun shone vigorously and felt quite warm in spite of the rather chilly east wind. There must have been a hundred people sitting on the grass in front of The Crooked Billet, or on deckchairs supplied free by the pub. Things have changed since the war (World War Two, that is) and it seems that the slightest glimmer of sunshine brings people out, particularly on the high streets where tables and chairs appear laden with coffee—from cafés and restaurants which simply weren't there in south east London where I lived—in those days. Nor did we drink much coffee, and few of us were lucky enough to travel then, but, with peace, mass air travel and tourism, people became used to eating—and drinking coffee— outside, in the sun!

Not, as I say, in Sydenham, but even so, my parents used to let me sleep in the back garden on hot summer nights and I remember how I lay under the huge apple tree (a Worcester Pearmain, I think) and heard trains clattering homewards and owls hooting. Often there were enormous thunderstorms and torrential rain which drove me back into the house.

28 March

'*Overdraven*' was a Dutch word used pejoratively about some people by my mother. (And enjoyed by Zena and me for all our years together.) I don't think it translates precisely. It's somewhere between exaggerated and mildly hysterical. Maybe in today's argot it would be OTT.

Anyway, what has put it in my mind is the reaction, especially in the media, to the terrorist attack on Westminster Bridge and the killing of PC Palmer at the entrance to Parliament. It isn't that I lack compassion for the unfortunate victims, slaughtered in such unlikely circumstances. No, it's probably my age and living a life in which death has played a not unusual part, which leads to my disparaging attitude. There seems something almost laughable about the rather self-congratulatory talk of keeping calm and carrying on. And at least one public figure explained how he intended to cross Westminster Bridge the very next day. What insouciance! What courage!

On the new £5 note there is Winston Churchill quoted: 'I have nothing to offer but blood, toil, tears and sweat.' Not quite our world, eh?

10 April

The two princes—William and Harry—have been involving themselves in the recognition and treatment of mental health. Harry has explained how his mother's death had—after some time—a shattering effect on his life. William has been a bit critical of the 'stiff upper lip'—our national way of facing difficulty. Odd really, that these two young chaps who have already seen combat in one case, and performed admirably as a helicopter rescuer in the other, should feel that way. Or perhaps I am the odd one in being surprised. My whole upbringing—from never 'blubbing' as a small boy to facing down problems later in life—demanded a positively glacial upper lip.

And I have always recalled (and amused my sons) by relating how my mother used to command me when (for example) stinging iodine was put on a grazed knee, to 'remember the wounded soldiers'.

15 April

Quick, quick! My finger flies to the off button on my radio. It is Thought for the Day and ... John Bell of the Iona Community. The mute button on my TV serves a similar purpose for—amongst others—a couple of Carolines (Lucas and Pigeon) and Tiny Tim Farron.

18 April

So, there's to be a 'snap' election. Pundits express surprise but I can't think why. If Mrs May wants to achieve the sort of majority she desires—and needs—she'll rarely have a better chance of getting one than now, with an ineffectual opposition. Also, the Brexit situation gives her a chance to gather in the UKIP voters (increasingly seen as the One Man Band minus the One Man). Moreover, a sizeable majority—approaching three figures, perhaps (but not much more, I hope), will enable her to keep her friends close and her enemies even closer, as they say.

30 April

Sunday morning and as usual at about 5:25 I start to listen to Radio 4. There's usually something mildly interesting on; and the general atmosphere and pleasant voices engender for me a calm (if not perilously soporific) mood. BOING! I spoke too soon for on comes 'Church Bells on Sunday'. After a quite interesting description of the age, location and number of bells comes the crashing clanging sound of Grandsire Temples or Cambridge Surprise Minor—names which mean nothing to me because—hard as I try—I can never discern any pattern to the dreadfully noisy intrusion on my Sunday morning peace.

I have to admit that I don't much like the sound of church bells, but I particularly dislike them early on a Sunday morning.

6 June

I am suddenly reminded that seventy-three (!) years ago today, I was sailing for Normandy on a choppy but sunlit English Channel. Hard to adjust to the idea of my younger self, tin-hatted against the incoming shellfire of the big German guns on the French coast. Mind you, I was comparatively elderly (twenty-six) compared to the young boys sent to Iraq, Helmand and other unsavoury places in recent times. Also, I had the experience of battle in the desert and Sicily to summon up the sinews or whatever it was one was supposed to do.

I've made no entry on the days of the terrorist killings in Manchester and London. This is partly because I find it difficult to reach any understanding of the people who become murderers in some totally irrational hate against our form of society. The hard fact which I cannot dispute in my own mind is that of all the world's major religions, only Islam has, in recent times, recruited followers who—admittedly in small numbers—can be 'radicalised' to kill those of other religions (or race) or of sexual lifestyles. Most extraordinary to me, is that young men who were born here as refugees, educated to university standards and who enjoyed all the zeitgeist pleasures and sports available to them, could be persuaded to kill innocent victims—and themselves—in the name of Allah. ('The most merciful, the most compassionate.') How to combat this? I simply don't know.

11 June

A few words about the General Election. Whatever her motives, I agreed with Mrs May's decision to call for one. However, I didn't agree with her Manifesto, which harped on irrelevances like fox-hunting, alienated core supporters, failed to clarify what is a reasonably sensible provision for assisted dying. And she had no ability at all to rub shoulders and shake hands with hoi polloi.

In this, she appears to have been completely outmanoeuvred by Mr Corbyn with his 'fully costed' totally unrealistic Manifesto and undisguised bribes for students—who (unsurprisingly) gave him a solid vote. Not that I wish to deprive students of their vote, but I think it should be in the form of a postal vote in their home constituency, not a great slab which distorts the vote in university towns.

To sum up: I think the Conservatives had a perfectly good record to defend, but signally failed to do so.

27 June

Last Saturday my usual evening TV diet on BBC4—vaguely unpleasant foreign thrillers—was not available. Why? Because the entire evening was given over to the Glastonbury Festival. Originally this was a fairly modest and primitive affair hosted by a farmer call Eavis and attended by young people who roughed it in little tents and usually ended up cheerfully covered in mud. Now, however, international 'stars' perform there. There are yurts and showers and notables such as Mr & Mrs Balls seen queuing up for a shower with their towels.

Anyway, accepting that Glastonbury is not for me, I tuned in for a few minutes before my bedtime. What did I see on the very big stage with its elaborate lighting? Father John Misty. This white person with a huge bushy beard and what looked like high heels glissaded about the stage, occasionally lying down, singing songs which were (for example) 'You are astride me' or 'you are inside me', which you might call fairly explicit—or for a change strumming his guitar and moaning oh-ooh-oh as he swooned about. Sometimes he raised his arms and swayed to and fro. The audience was lighted up and I could see hundreds (thousands!) of (it seemed) young girls, arms aloft and moaning oh-ooh-oh just like 'Father John'.

Before I became too censorious, I reminded myself that when I was younger there was a crooner Johnny 'Cry' Ray at whom a multitude of small girls screamed and threw their knickers. Not so much 'new under the sun' then?

11 July

I eat British strawberries on most days as soon as they appear. There is a particularly abundant crop this year but I do find that the berries are rather large and not as full of flavour as once (it seems). I think it's my failing taste buds as nothing seems to appeal to them much nowadays. I remember when I was young we used to buy strawberries loose by the bag, costing, I think about ninepence a pound. My father, who had an entirely misplaced belief in the powers of white bread, insisted on mashing strawberries as a bread and butter sandwich, which ruined them for us. We had to take to eating them secretly when Pa wasn't home—which was most of the time. Maybe it's unfair to relate this detail about him when I also remember how he used to bring delicious and luxurious fruit from Salmon & Gluckstein's stall at London Bridge station on his way home every Saturday lunchtime when he completed his five and a half day working week.

1 August

There's been much media coverage of the twentieth anniversary of the death of Princess Diana. I have always thought—and this might come as a bit of a surprise—that the best thing she did was to die young. Best for her because she leaves a picture of youth and beauty and the belief, whether wholly true or not, in one wronged and mistreated, with her totally unsuitable entanglements forgiven—or forgotten.

It's best certainly for the Royal Family who would have been harried by a loose cannon and a potential threat to the ascent to the throne of Prince Charles. And to us—the public—best because we can expect a smooth transition to the throne untroubled by civil disturbance. My abiding memories of Diana are of the shy early virgin and the later avenging beauty. And she remains firmly in credit with me when I see the TV picture of her and her boys shrieking with excitement as they plunge down the water chute amid clouds of spray. The boys are her major achievement—a couple of good eggs—particularly the one-time rascal, Harry. I think that I warm to her over them because she reminds me of the way Zena brought up my own two sons, that mixture of love and total involvement.

24 September

'NOW' announces Kim, my delightful (Filipina?) nurse, 'I CLEAN YOUR BUM'—having already strip-washed my cringing old body. To quote from elsewhere: 'As a sheep before its shearers is dumb, so he opened not his mouth'. Bum? Sheep? What the hell is this man going on about? Yes, perhaps I should have mentioned that I had just fallen (been tripped?) in Waitrose and broken my left hip. (I feel that my elder sister Elly might have said 'Well it might have been worse, you could have done it in Morrisons.')

Anyway, I plunged to the floor and could not rise. An ambulance was summoned and morphine supplied several times by mouth before I arrived at Kingston Hospital. Called on my mobile, my wonderful neighbour, Camilla, advised the boys, collected my car, and took everything off my hands. By the time Richard arrived at the hospital, the morphine must have made me a bit goofy as I apparently insisted that I was being treated in Hawaii. Anyway, I was x-rayed and next morning (a hip break being confirmed) operated on using an epidural, so that, apart from the rather alarming drilling and banging, I emerged successful and—once again, indebted to the NHS.

28 September

It's difficult to get down to writing again, but I should add a few notes about the following days. My previous in-patient spells had been at St George's, a larger and possibly better hospital in terms of facilities etc. than Kingston. However, I found the atmosphere in Kingston more friendly and personal. Everyone was on first name terms. Nurses were all named and helpful (and unruffled by my early attempt to use the urine 'bottle' which resulted in wet pyjama trousers.) The bottle was a large plastic thing with a very large aperture into which my little nurse, Abigail, told me I should put my 'baby'. In the event, I gave up, which meant that I mastered my Zimmer frame more quickly as I shuffled across to the loo.

It must have been a dozen years since I was in hospital and I was immediately struck by how much the food had improved. Two printed daily menus ('Main lunch' and 'Light supper') allowed you a choice of twenty or so dishes, which, when they appeared, were quite tasty and warm.

Trussed up as I was, sleeping was not easy and most nights saw me—I am ashamed to admit—weeping gently at 3 a.m. in the darkened ward. 'Please don't let me die here,' I pleaded with some unknown presence.

Things were quiet by then, though earlier the silence had been broken by a patient (never actually seen) who came in shortly after me and bellowed continually. 'Help, help,' he would shout. (Eventually he was put in a side room and pacified except for occasional outbursts.) I called him the Tree Howler, like the vociferous monkeys I'd seen on TV. Another notable I christened 'The Emperor' as he (frequently) pushed his Zimmer frame to the loo. (When I told Richard this, he immediately responded 'Haile Selassie' so I suppose there must have been some echo from the 1930s and the Abyssinian war.)

9 October

We are told—almost daily it seems—that we are, as a nation, obese. And, indeed, shopping in a supermarket, you often find yourself impeded by an enormous backside or a pendulous beer belly escaping from inadequate trousers. A podgy child will often be in tow, pausing to collect sweets or crisps or whatever seems to contribute to its increasing rotundity.

How almost baffling this situation seemed to me when one afternoon last week, the first three programmes I idly surfed on the TV were all devoted to food or cooking. There were the frantic competitors, chopping, boiling etc., and the judges munching and slurping as the juices ran down their chin (or, sometimes, chins).

It does seem as though we are almost obsessively interested in food. And, I think, you are what you eat. Hence a fatter nation.

Mind you, I'm a hypocrite for writing the above because when Maria is away I'm fed by Claire, a professional chef, and what a treat it is. Leftover bits of chicken appear in a delectable sauce and everything is piping hot. I watch her at work and marvel. Still, I don't eat large meals, so I'm not obese. And, at 99, unlikely to become so.

19 October

A mere handful of weeks ago I felt some pride as I managed to totter, clutching my Zimmer frame, to the pillar box about fifty yards over the road. Today I did half my daily walk (now measured by Anneke, my lovely young carer, at three quarters of a mile, not the half mile I had guessed.) So, guided by my physiotherapist, Natasha, I have, over the two-plus months since I've come home, made steady progress. First pushing my wheelie to the end of Wright's Alley. Then (a bit of an effort) my whole journey with the wheelie (about 25 minutes), accompanied by Anneke or another carer. Why, then, the excitement over today's half walk? Because—as encouraged by Natasha—I did the journey with *one stick* as in the days before I became such an old wreck. Admittedly I had to switch to my wheelie at half way, and arrived home with aching back, arms and shoulders. But I am in sight of the target I set myself when I left hospital, which was, one day, to resume my daily walk. By 1st November perhaps?

23 October

Red Letter Day. I completed my whole walk with just one stick, not quite as easily as with the formerly unbroken limb but very satisfying. And my carer was proud of me!

31 October

The other day I watched a commercial on TV where the presenter proudly showed a box which would record no fewer than six separate programmes while permitting you to watch a seventh at the same time. I thought to myself: but who would want such a thing which would involve spending so much of your life watching telly?

Then—before I became *too* censorious—I thought I'd just check up on my own viewing, compared if I was able to find it out, with the national average. So, here's a more or less accurate picture of my weekday diet (I'll deal with Sunday later).

12.00–1.30: Daily Politics and News	1½ hours
6.00–6.30: Rather deplorable Oz soap	
used in the past for Zena at supper time	½ hour
8.00–8.30: *EastEnders*	½ hour
9.00–10.00 Selected programme	1 hour
	Total: 3½ hours

Plus, on Saturdays racing 1.30–4.00.	
Soccer results 4.30–5.00	3½ hours
Plus, Test match highlights on 5 when applicable	1 hour
Sundays some recorded football at Richard's	
and something worthwhile in evening	2 hours.

So I seem to average about 240 minutes a day—more to my chagrin than the national average of 217 (in itself only tenth among the leading nations, headed by USA at 274).

Mind you, I'm not knocking TV when I think what was on offer in my youth—maybe a visit to 'the flicks' once a week. Now a world is opened to us by programmes like Blue Planet, when a mere eighty or so years ago, the Prime Minister was able to refer to Czechoslovakia as 'a far away country of which we know nothing'.

I always remember my best friend Mervyn, who in the early days of TV was asked what he liked on television. 'Everything,' he replied.

1 November

A rather gruelling session with Natasha, who regards me as 98% recovered from my breakage. The remaining 2% seems to be concentrated on my backache, which has made the last two walks a bit of an ordeal. Still, think of a couple of months back; and be grateful.

4 December

On 7 September, back home from hospital, I asked my physiotherapist whether I should ever be able to do my daily walk again. I would, she assured me. And yesterday a rather gloomy Sunday saw me complete my ¾ mile alone for the first time since I broke my hip. I went to bed last night satisfied; and a bit tired.

6 December

Today is the fourth year since I brought Mina home with me. A truism, I know, but she has become a very large presence in my life from the morning moment when I cry 'doods' and she flies downstairs, to the turning off of my bedside light and 'assuming the position' in readiness for the stealthy paw across my pillow and her warm body leaning against me as I slide towards sleep.

31 December

I have delayed (avoided?) writing about the burdens of life in very old age because I am filled with guilt at my sad, grumbling mood—a struggle, in fact, against the depression which has already struck me twice in life.

I have so little to grumble about when I compare my life to that of many unfortunates around the world, fighting just to survive in places like Syria and Bangladesh. And not only so far afield. Thousands of our own fellow citizens have to huddle in shop doorways or other corners of the cold pavement each night with their solitary blanket or duvet, struggling to sleep, hungry and dispossessed.

Compared to these luckless people, the trials of my daily life are, indeed, trivial. Yet as I struggle to put on my socks or shoes—something done in a few seconds just a short time ago—I do feel diminished. And when I go for my daily walk, hobbling along with my stout stick, I notice how everyone else seems to stride out so quickly, so effortlessly.

Things are out of reach and I am afraid to stand on a chair to get at them. (In any case, I've promised my sons that I won't). I am clumsy, drop things, bump into things. I move slowly, uncertainly; every morning I face a real battle to leave the warmth and security of my bed. Since I broke my hip (now quite recovered so why am I moaning?) I have had a firm of private carers, discovered by Richard, looking after me. It has become a luxury (which started as a necessity) which I am reducing during January and then giving up altogether. I shall miss my lovely South African carer, Anneke, who—as I've told her—has become like a granddaughter to me and who, from the time she brings in my breakfast, makes everything in my life so much easier.

So, as I say, I have really very little to grumble about. Kind neighbours keep an eye on me and I'm still able to walk my ¾ mile every day (albeit with an aching back) and drive (not too large distances) in my trusty Clio.

When I complain to friends and family they remind me that (plot spoiler!) I shall be a hundred years old on the Ides of March, now only three months away. As I tell them, whatever the calendar may say, inside yourself you are the same creature as you always were, which is, I suppose, why I bang on about my trivial troubles. A new year starts tomorrow. Nearly a hundred years ago, Britain faced some dark days as the fifth army was defeated and nearly destroyed by the last great German offensive of the First World War. And in a small Sussex seaside town a child was soon to be born to fight in a second world war; and to survive into this very old age. It seems a good time to give some sort of thanks.